PHYLLIS TICKLE

MODERN SPIRITUAL MASTERS SERIES

PHYLLIS TICKLE

Essential Spiritual Writings

Edited and with an Introduction by

JON M. SWEENEY

ORBIS BOOKS
Maryknoll, New York 10545

Founded in 1970, Orbis Books endeavors to publish works that enlighten the mind, nourish the spirit, and challenge the conscience. The publishing arm of the Maryknoll Fathers and Brothers, Orbis seeks to explore the global dimensions of the Christian faith and mission, to invite dialogue with diverse cultures and religious traditions, and to serve the cause of reconciliation and peace. The books published reflect the views of their authors and do not represent the official position of the Maryknoll Society. To learn more about Maryknoll and Orbis Books, please visit our website at www.maryknollsociety.org.

Published by Orbis Books, Box 302, Maryknoll, NY 10545-0302.

Manufactured in the United States of America

Tickle, Phyllis.
[Works. Selections. 2015]
Phyllis Tickle : essential spiritual writings / selected with an introduction by Jon M. Sweeney.
pages cm. -- (Modern spiritual masters series)
Includes bibliographical references and index.
ISBN 978-1-62698-137-9
I. Sweeney, Jon M., 1967- editor. II. Title. III. Title: Essential spiritual writings.
BX4827.T495A25 2015 248--dc23

Contents

Sources

This is not a complete author bibliography, but the following published works are quoted and/or cited in the selections that follow.

The Story of Two Johns. Memphis, TN: St. Luke's Press, 1976. [Fiction]

Selections. National Library of Pocket Poets. Notre Dame, IN: Erasmus Books of Notre Dame, 1983.

The Tickle Papers: Parables and Pandemonium. Nashville: Abingdon Press, 1987. [Essays]

Re-Discovering the Sacred: Spirituality in America. New York: Crossroad Publishing Company, 1995.

God-Talk in America. New York: Crossroad Publishing Company, 1998.

The Shaping of a Life: A Spiritual Landscape. New York: Doubleday, 2003.

What the Land Already Knows: Winter's Sacred Days. Chicago: Loyola Press, 2003. [First published under the same title by the Upper Room, Nashville, 1985.]

Greed: The Seven Deadly Sins. New York: Oxford University Press, 2004.

The Graces We Remember: Sacred Days of Ordinary Time. Chicago: Loyola Press, 2004. [First published as *Ordinary Time: Stories of the Days between Ascensiontide and Advent*. Nashville: Upper Room, 1988.]

Wisdom in the Waiting: Spring's Sacred Days. Chicago: Loyola Press, 2004. [First published as *Final Sanity: Stories of Lent, Easter, and the Great Fifty Days*. Nashville: Upper Room, 1987.]

Prayer Is a Place: America's Religious Landscape Observed. New York: Doubleday, 2005.

The Great Emergence: How Christianity Is Changing and Why. Grand Rapids, MI: Baker Books, 2008.

The Words of Jesus: A Gospel of the Sayings of Our Lord; With Reflections by Phyllis Tickle. San Francisco: Jossey-Bass, 2008.

Acknowledgments

Many people have helped to make this book come to fruition. My sincerest thanks go to Michael Lawrence, sales manager at Orbis Books, for his early enthusiasm. Thanks also to Joseph Durepos, Phyllis Tickle's long-time agent and friend, for help in obtaining permissions. Both Catherine Kramer and Chad Allen at Baker Books were helpful in obtaining and granting permission to reprint material, as was my friend Gary Jansen at Image Books/Random House. Old school, good guy publishing people, all of them!

I made frequent use of the work of Tony Jones and Kelly Piggott, as I frequently referred to their editor's introduction and annotated bibliography, respectively, in *Phyllis Tickle: Evangelist of the Future* (Paraclete Press, 2014). Thanks to the two of them.

Who would this book be dedicated to but Phyllis Tickle herself? I am proud to call her a friend.

For those with a scholarly interest in the work of Phyllis Tickle, her complete papers are housed at the Livingston Library, Shorter University, Rome, Georgia.

Phyllis Tickle's Life and Work: A Chronological Overview

1934 Phyllis Natalie Alexander born March 12 to Philip Wade Alexander and Katherine Ann Porter Alexander. Spends most of childhood in Johnson City, Tennessee, where her father is dean of East Tennessee State University.

1951 Enrolls at Shorter College, Rome, Georgia, at seventeen on full academic scholarship. Later transfers to East Tennessee State.

1955 Graduates East Tennessee State. In June, marries Samuel Milton Tickle, whom she first met "when he was exactly thirteen months old and I exactly six weeks . . . in the newborn nursery at First Presbyterian Church in Johnson City."[1] In September, begins teaching Latin and English in the Memphis public schools.

1958 Moves with Sam and their two children to Pelzer, South Carolina, where Sam works as a rural country doctor.

1961 Earns Master of Arts, Furman University. The family moves to Memphis.

1962–65 Instructor, Memphis College of Art; Lecturer, Rhodes College.

1965–71 Dean of humanities, Memphis College of Art.

1971 In late May, gives birth to a second son, Philip Wade Alexander Tickle, their fifth child, who tragically and violently dies of pneumonia two weeks later. Phyllis

1. *The Shaping of a Life,* 84.

	later describes "almost anesthetizing grief."
1972	Launches St. Luke's Press, a small publishing house, with friends and colleagues from the Memphis College of Art. Also teaches poetry for the Tennessee Arts Commission and begins publishing poems in magazines and journals. Gives birth to the last of her seven children.
1974	First book, a chancel drama about the Hebrew prophet Jeremiah, *Figs and Fury*, is published.
1977	The family moves to The Farm in Lucy, the subject of much of Tickle's oeuvre.
1977–87	Poet in Residence, Memphis Brooks Museum of Art.
1983	*Selections*, a new and selected volume of poems.
1989	St. Luke's Press is purchased by Peachtree Publishers in Atlanta; Tickle is retained as senior editor. Two years later, she retires from active publishing.
1992	Recruited by *Publishers Weekly* to be founding religion editor of the trade journal.
1995	*Re-Discovering the Sacred: Spirituality in America*, her first book-length work on the phenomenon that was the burgeoning of interest in religion and spirituality in the 1990s. *God-Talk in America* follows in 1997.
2000	*Prayers for Summertime,* the first volume of *The Divine Hours,* is published in February, marking the beginning of a decade devoted to exploring the deep, ancient roots of her Christian faith.
2001	*The Shaping of a Life: A Spiritual Landscape,* her autobiography, published in April.

2004 Retires from *Publishers Weekly*.

2004 Receives honorary Doctor of Humane Letters from Berkeley School of Divinity at Yale University.

2008 *The Great Emergence: How Christianity Is Changing and Why* is published and becomes a rapid success. Tickle becomes the recognized historian of Emergence Christianity.

2009 Receives honorary Doctor of Humane Letters from North Park University. Continues to lecture, often traveling forty weeks a year.

2014 Celebrates eightieth birthday in Denver, Colorado, at the Christianity21 Conference, and at Fuller Seminary in Anaheim, California, during the public launch of a Festschrift edited by Tony Jones and published in her honor. Retires from active traveling and public speaking.

2015 Death of her husband, Dr. Samuel M. Tickle, Sr., on January 2 in Memphis. Phyllis continues living on The Farm in Lucy, still writing—mostly poetry.

Introduction
Rare Tickle

Phyllis Tickle is not exactly famous on the world stage, but her reputation on this continent as a spiritual writer, religion journalist, and independent scholar of the religious past, present, and future is first-rate. She has been an active, published author for half a century. Furthermore, to describe her in much the same way that people once talked about Billy Graham, Tickle has surely lectured and preached to more people over the last quarter century than any other woman in America with the possible exceptions of Sister Joan Chittister and Sister Helen Prejean. Good company.

Tickle has earned her place as one of the modern spiritual masters of the late twentieth and early twenty-first centuries. And just as Sisters Joan and Helen are Roman Catholic yet their audiences have not at all been limited to Catholics, Tickle's readership quickly transcends her Episcopalianism. Raised Presbyterian, she first fell in love with Anglican liturgy, prayer, and practice during college, and other than a brief period of time when first married, she has remaining devoted to that path all of her life.

But one doesn't have to be Episcopalian to be stirred by her expressions of faith. There is a universal quality to her passions for religious language and its potential to form and transform a life. For example, there is a moment in her autobiography when Tickle remembers her first experience of Morning Prayer and the Book of Common Prayer:

> I don't think I had ever known God *was*, until that Sunday . . . I don't think I had ever envisioned a being that was other than all-present, all-powerful, and handy as a shirt pocket to have around. . . . I . . . don't mean to suggest that I now know how to catch with words that

> something that is beyond catching. But I do mean to say that months later, in first-year Greek, I would be assigned "*En arche ein o Logos, kai o Logos ein pros ton Theon, kai o Logos o Theos ein.*" "In the beginning was the Word and the Word was with God, and the word was God." And I would physically and rather violently suck in my breath and then tear up because I did understand enough by then to recognize what they were.[2]

She is a Christian and an Episcopalian, yes, but as you will soon see, other writings in this volume show her expressing similar emotions in the context of observing, and even experiencing, the faith of others.

Tickle's oeuvre has evolved through five chronological periods, from poet to essayist to journalist of religion ("sociologist of religion as it is commercially applied," she once called it[3]) to evangelist for fixed-hour prayer, and finally, to popular historian of Emergence. Over the course of these genres and aspects of her career, her vocation has always been to the struggle to come to terms with what it means to live a life with and for God.

Her career has followed a similar trajectory to her writing. She's taken turns as academic, book publisher, freelance writer, religion journalist, and then, finding her greatest commercial success as a writer with *The Divine Hours* series of volumes, and her various prognostications of Emergence Christianity, most of all *The Great Emergence*. It is these works of the last fifteen years that 95 percent of Tickle's current readers know her for. For this reason, the present volume aims to introduce you to what one might call "Rare Tickle"—the substantial, important, yet rarely seen work of her long career.

Chances are good that more than half of what you'll read in this book you have never read before, even if you have been an avid reader of Tickle's work for many years. This is because her writing has spanned nearly three generations, but most of her

2. Ibid., 45.

3. The *Great Emergence*, 11.

current readers know her only for the major books published since 2000. As one example of what is unique to this volume, you will soon see examples of her fine poetry. In fact, the poems that I've chosen—written ten to twenty years before Tickle's tenure as the founding editor in religion at *Publishers Weekly*—aim to demonstrate how the themes of her life and work have been consistent for half a century.

In *The Shaping of a Life*, her autobiography, Tickle was dismissive of her poetry (quoting husband, Sam, to that effect), calling it youthful work. She then commented, "[I]f I failed as a poet because of having no more than a modest talent for it, I most certainly did not fail for any lack of trying. I left behind me, as a matter of fact, a whole trail of poetry, every line of it, so far as I can remember, true to its times as fully confessional."[4] But over the last few years, my conversations with Tickle have convinced me that she no longer sees the poetry of her thirties and forties in this light. Today she properly values it, and is, in fact, returning to the writing of poetry now, in her eighties.

Tickle's poetic work seems to fulfill a pregnant promise that Seamus Heaney had for poets and good poems, as expressed in his Nobel lecture in 1995:

> There are times when a deeper need enters, when we want the poem to be not only pleasurably right but compellingly wise, not only a surprising variation played upon the world, but a returning of the world to itself. We want the surprise to be transitive, like the impatient thump which unexpectedly restores the picture to the television set, or the electric shock which sets the fibrillating heart back to its proper rhythm.

Many readers may be surprised by the poetry. I hope so.

There are several spiritual themes that lurk consistently in Tickle's poems, as in her essays, theological reflections, histories, and analyses of the age in which we live. For the sake of pulling a book together, I have identified these as "Surprise and Wonder,"

4. *The Shaping of a Life*, 25.

"Stories and Sins," "Prayer—Fixed-Hour and Otherwise," "The Great Emergence," and "The Old, Old Story." If you feel that you thoroughly know her writing on one of these topics, I hope and believe you'll still find something here that you haven't seen before. Also, it goes without saying that a different five themes might just as easily have been chosen. Perhaps they will, if we ever follow this volume with another.

There are many recurring emotions throughout these spiritual writings, as well. You may, for instance, be surprised how often Tickle reflects on loss, death, and the opacity of the veil between life here and the life to come. This is a woman who knows what it means to live deliberately and who has deeply experienced death, as well. She gave birth to seven children and has written and spoken about the pain of several miscarriages. She also suffered the death of a son just two weeks after his birth. These experiences both inform and arise in what follows. In addition, Tickle's husband, Sam, was a longtime rural family physician who often witnessed death firsthand. And together, Phyllis and Sam lived and raised their family on a farm, where slaughtering animals that had been lovingly raised, and even named, was a natural part of life. An essay on this last topic is one of my favorite bits, below in chapter 1.

Let us also note that Phyllis Tickle is a Southern writer. To my knowledge, this has not been pointed out before, and I don't propose to take the space, here, to do so in detail. But one experiences throughout her writings a tone and perspective that stands alien to what one might call a more Northern (or even, Californian) cheeriness, progress, and gesturing to enlightenment that has characterized so much spiritual writing of the last two generations. Instead of progress, Tickle often points to virtue, and she clearly values taking risks. Instead of optimism, she articulates a Christian hope; and she often ends an essay in the kind of mystery that, by definition, eschews any clear or simple conclusion.

Tickle also stands apart from the simplifying "life as pilgrimage" mode of diagnosing the human condition. In this sense, I see the body of her writing in Faulknerian terms. Just for fun, let me point out that both writers grew up in university towns in the American South, Tickle in Johnson City, Tennessee, Faulkner in Oxford, Mississippi. The essential setting of much of Tickle's prose, The Farm in Lucy, is about as far north of Memphis as Faulkner's mythical Yoknapatawpha County is south of the city in northern Mississippi. But, more important, Faulkner said in his 1950 Nobel acceptance speech (one year before Phyllis went off to college) that the only subject worth writing about is "the human heart in conflict with itself." Had it not already been the novelist's idea, such a phrase would have made a good title for this volume of the writings of Phyllis Tickle.

I have read and reread most of what Tickle has written, I am sure, and have never come across a reference to William Faulkner in her work. However, I'm guessing that the novels and short stories were an essential part of her early schooling, and I see the stalking and menace of "The Bear" in much of Tickle's attempts to come to terms with the essentially and elusively spiritual in the world about her.

This shows up most often on The Farm in Lucy, the central character in her essays. In that very real place, she never simply communes with nature—there is no easiness in what she writes—but she comes to understand natural things, even enough to struggle with them. The characters in a Faulkner novel do the same, fighting with the land as with themselves. And then there is the way in which family unites, divides, and challenges a solitary soul, as it so palpably does in a good Faulkner novel, as in a good Tickle essay.

Above all, Tickle is a passionate writer. Whether she is acting as sociologist of religion, essayist on the meaning of the spiritual life, or creator of accessible fixed-hour prayer, she packs a punch. Passion sometimes comes early in a piece; other times, it is tucked at the end. But a fervent faith abides in all that she writes. That is surely why she has the following of readers that she does. And Tickle never leaves a subject—even her historical sweeps, of which there are a few in the pages to come—without expressing herself in personal terms that resonate with any person of any faith.

The faith communicated in all of her work is never simply Christian. Tickle is in company with those who see and understand other traditions and practices so clearly because they are deeply rooted in their own. The passion and the writing are bound together, as when she reflected on witnessing whirling dervishes for the first time in her capacity as a journalist: "When I had started to cry, I do not know. It didn't matter. I had never seen ecstatic worship before, never understood before that the human body is light and its God a consuming fire from which it emanates and to which it returns with erotic ferocity when it frees itself to know itself. . . . Islam, by whatever name, was no longer a theory."[5] That, after all, is how she captures our attention.

Now, a couple of housekeeping notes. First, all footnotes are Phyllis Tickle's, not my own. In most cases, they were originally published as endnotes, attached to the text in question. But since there are so few of them—and I have retained only a few—here they are reproduced as footnotes. Second, whereas Tickle frequently employs ellipses for emphasis in her writing, I have replaced these with what copyeditors call the em dash (—) in order to distinguish a punctuation mark of emphasis from an editorial mark used to signify content passed over in the midst of a quotation.

Jon M. Sweeney

5. *Prayer Is a Place*, 63.

1

Surprise and Wonder

The Cranes

Where along their migratory way
these cranes may also stop
I can not say.
The river's a dozen miles from here
but twice, sometimes more,
each year
they drop,
a fleet of sails
on a sea
of grass,
like manna and the quails
come from some other land
to say,
"This way! This way!"

—*Selections*

* * *

This first section includes excerpts from essays of the 1970s through the early years of the 2000s about the everyday blessings and essential sacredness of life. Included are passages from a trilogy of books, first written and published thirty years ago, devoted to spiritual understandings gleaned from living by the rhythms of the land; these show Tickle in step with the early influential writings of Wendell Berry. As she explains in this chapter, "Religion has always kept earth time. Liturgy only gives sanction to what the heart already knows."

And yet, we don't begin on The Farm in Lucy, but with the more familiar voice of Tickle, well known to her readers over the last decade and a half—writing theologically and philosophically about the importance of remembering who we are, by asking and re-asking the most basic questions, and considering the earliest story of them all.

IN THE BEGINNING, EDEN

One of the genuine pleasures of the writing life, ironically enough, is not writing at all; rather, it is the business of speaking directly and in real time to audiences. For a writer like me who is by area of expertise a professional religionist, those audiences usually are made up of other religionists, most commonly of practicing clergy, their professional support staffs, deeply involved and committed laity, or any combination of these. But sometimes, and blessedly, the audience is an auditorium full of undergraduates, and the occasion an endowed lecture of one sort or another.

At such events, the initial attitude in the meeting hall is almost always exactly what anybody would expect from eighteen- and nineteen- and twenty-year-olds who have been told, firmly and at least three times, that this is a required event and they had better show for it. The truth is, however, that most young adults cannot manage to stay aloof and uninvolved for more than about three minutes, especially when they are assembled in aggregate. After that, curiosity and strong opinions and just plain joie de vivre kick in, and you've got them.

As a result and as any writer will tell you, it's these lectures that are devoutly to be desired; for while one always learns something in any public engagement with any audience, what one learns in the course of engaging a healthy, lively undergraduate audience is, more often than not, opinion-changing and mind-expanding. More to the point, it always and unfailingly gives birth to at least one poignant story or one simple but brilliant insight or one gentle conviction still too new to be tarnished by over-much handling. Sometimes, though very rarely, an endowed lecture will deliver up all three in one fell swoop. I had one of those rare experiences recently.

I was giving a set of endowed lectures at an urban college in the Midwest. In this particular case, the audience, while primarily undergraduates, had a few graduate students and seminarians thrown in, probably just for flavor, more than anything else. But their presence in the lecture hall and their active participation in the question-and-answer sessions after each lecture placed a kind of restraint or false decorum on the collegians whom I had hoped to engage in genuine exchange. While I was delighted to hear from the older students, I nonetheless went into the concluding lecture with less intellectual anticipation and excitement than is usually the case at the end of a series of talks.

When the talk and the question-and-answer session were over, a few students and faculty gathered, as they always do, around the podium to carry the discussion into a more personal and candid wind-down. But one of those who came that last afternoon was quite clearly an undergraduate and, I thought, most probably a freshman. From her self-effacement and decorum of earnest unease, I guessed as well that college had been her first, intimate experience of life in the city.

She had two other students with her, and together they hung back, listening to the discussion and waiting until everyone else had drifted away. The three of them seemed to be very close in affection and also in concern, but my freshman was obviously their leader and spokeswoman. Could they ask me one last question, she wanted to know. I said of course, and almost immediately realized that what she wanted to express was not so much a question as it was the perfect self-articulation I had come here hoping to receive.

What she actually said was, "I want somebody to tell me where I stop." She shrugged her shoulders, and the boy in the group poked her to go on. She tried again. "What I mean is that I don't know any more where I end."

"Am I just inside my skin, sort of interior to it, you know? Or am I just what's on the inside side of my underwear and clothes.

Or am I as far out as my aura," because, she added rather apologetically, "there really is an aura around all of us, or so our psych prof says anyway."

"Or am I, like, only just here in amongst us three, because we really do hang together all the time?"

"Or am I out in all of this?" and she gave a kind of feeble but all-encompassing sweep of her hand toward the auditorium behind us. Then she shrugged, almost in defeat, and there was a kind of break in her voice.

"I just want to know where I stop, that's all—where I aren't any more."

I don't know whether it was her earnestness or her slip into colloquialism that most endeared that girl-child to me in that moment; but either way, there was no doubting the sincerity of her desire to be answered. One can say, and accurately so, that what she was asking was basically an existential question. But one must also say, and again accurately, that her existential experience was as valid as it was painful. On the farm—it turned out to be a dairy farm, by the way—she had known where she stopped. She didn't, in other words. That is, on the farm, she simply did not "stop."

As far as the eye could see and as far as the imagination could reach, she was; for she and the earth by whose rules she lived were part and parcel of one another. She rose in accord with her father's cows who rose in accord with the demands of their milk making. She tended animals in accord with the seasons of both the earth and of their bodies which were part of it; and the ebb and flow of both of those determined the ebb and flow of her own. She knew herself to be no more than a cog in a magnificent machine, but she knew the machine was immense and total and that, by function and connection, she was totally vulnerable, ultimately powerless and because of those things totally borderless. She was, in effect, the quintessential expression of a rural understanding of earth.

I, too, am rural. Or like my young inquisitor, I once lived rural and still think rural. The farm we worked and ate off of for years was beef, not dairy, and family-size small, not working size large. And though my husband and I still live on a considerable portion of that same land, we no longer make any pretense of farming it. Our barn molders away in the hot west Tennessee sun, each passing season taking a bit more of its paint or its siding or, of recent years, its tin roofing. No cows have grazed our fields in over a decade, and only bush hogging keeps our pastures open now. The kitchen garden still feeds us well in the summers, but I no longer make any pretense of preserving and canning or freezing back against the winter's short supplies. Without children to feed and without children to teach, it seems pointless. They learned while they were with us and while they ate the product of their own hands. Like us, they still think rural, even though some of our seven no longer live that way.

What, then, would I or mine say now about the business—the habits and mind-sets and emotions—of thinking rural? First and always, when faced with that question, I interrupt to say that, in America especially, one must never use the expression "thinking rural" casually or without annotation. For a people whose immediate forebears were almost all farm-bound in lifestyle and income, and for a nation whose land mass is huge and mostly farmed or kept fallow, twenty-first century Americans have an almost paradoxical tendency to romanticize rurality. And once something is romanticized, it is effectually relegated to the precious and away from the operative and informing.

There is nothing romantic or even particularly ennobling about getting welts all over one's hands from picking okra and corn, or bruises from being jostled by hungry cows, or stiff bones from shoveling manure. What there is, however, is that subtle but pervasive sense of citizenship in the world as it is. What there is is the borderlessness of my freshman, her humanizing acceptance of vulnerability, and her assumption of oneness in substance and rhythm with the immediate environment, immediate being defined for her as a certain, unimpeded vastness that she could walk freely upon.

The shock for the rural thinker turned city dweller is in discovering that the city lives, not on the Earth, but above it by several layers of mechanical and technological remove. The urban dweller (who quickly becomes an urban thinker), uses the treasures of the Earth not to perpetuate and preserve it, but to serve and facilitate the life of the city. The rural thinker stands small in a grandeur he or she must accommodate to constantly. The urban thinker stands on a stage he or she has cut to size and then, standing there, dares to write the play.

Neither side of that divide in thinking and perceiving is inherently superior to, or worse than, the other. There is nothing quaint or impractical or regressive about rural values any more than there is anything malevolent or noxious or destructive about urbanization per se. In point of fact, condemning postmodern urban life is in many ways just another, albeit more negative, form of romanticization, and just as deplorable.

Likewise, there is not anything fundamentally deleterious to a human being about having to make the existential shifts required in moving from rural to urban living. What is wrong is our current inability or outright unwillingness to balance, meld, and employ simultaneously both ways of seeing the Earth and addressing the environment. Embedded in the earnestness of our current concerns is a kind of partisan entrenchment on both sides. Each hesitates to make a place at the table for much discussion of the differences which accrue between addressing conservation and ecology with intent to govern them and addressing them with intent to be as one with them. But for me, as a practicing Christian as well as a professional religionist, environmental arguments based on common sense or enlightened self-interest will always be, at best, secondary or tertiary ones.

When I say I am a practicing Christian, what I am saying, among other things, is that like a large part of the Earth's population—the larger part, in fact—I am what technically is called an Abrahamic, or, put another way, a member of the Abrahamic faiths. That is, Jews, Christians, and Muslims alike all claim a common spiritual forebear in Abraham. As such, we hold in common the part of Torah which is the story of human experience from the creation itself to Abraham's call to sacrifice his son to God. In that foundational bit of shared religious heritage, the dominant stories for us are the opening and closing ones—the Creation and the aborted Sacrifice. In both stories, a great gift is given to humanity and an order to be reverenced is established. It is the ordering of the Torah creation story, however, which every observant Abrahamic, whether farmer, suburbanite, or industrialist, is called to honor first when he or she speaks about environmental issues.

For Abrahamics, the great gift in Eden was that of receiving soul, of our birthing as creatures formed in the image of God. But there was a prior gift which enabled the great gift. There was Eden. Only after God's forming of a context for the soul's well-being, were *we* formed.

Both the rural and the urban dweller recognize, albeit in different ways, that creation is a tool, a gift to be enjoyed, and a means to be employed; but for the observant Jew or Christian or Muslim, the Earth exists neither to be deified nor to be consumed. Rather, it exists now, as it has from the beginning, as teacher, limitation, and purposed circumstance. It is a nursery of sorts, an incubator, in which each of us may first uncurl, then stretch, and finally rise up into the business of growing holy before God. Whatever we plot to do with and to the Earth is always to be measured by what pursuing such an action will do to human souls and their progress toward living fully into the image of God. And I would submit that, in the final analysis, such a gauge is the only sustainable one, simply because it alone is a benison upon all God's peoples, whether they be Abrahamic or not.

—written for The Sierra Club and published by them in *Holy Ground: A Gathering of Voices on Caring for Creation*, edited by Lyndsay Moseley and the staff of Sierra Club Books, 2008.

* * *

Tickle often writes philosophically, and these ruminations are frequently poetic, with a deep sense of wonder. On these occasions, she seems to write not only to instruct, but to move and inspire. Here are two examples.

THE SACRED IS OUR TRUE HOME

The sacred is a structural given in our being, very much indeed like one's cardiovascular system or the sun that for so many human eons has served as symbol to the sacred. Like those things, the sacred can be perceived but never embraced, for it and they are as fundamentally and inextricably woven into life as its perfume is into a flower or its meaning is into a word. Yet just as we know ourselves to have moved into and through the perfume of the sweet spring daffodils or to have named and passed on an articulated idea, so too we know when we have "moved" into the sacred, for the sacred is most frequently referenced by us as geography.

It is the words and metaphors of place with which we discuss the sacred and by means of which we see ourselves as able to engage it; although at the very moment in which we speak of that "otherness" as another world, we know in ourselves the hollowness of such a naming, for the sacred is "place" as no Earth place is. Like the womb that we cannot remember, the sacred is itself. Its placeness is its aliveness, and all our words are thereby frustrated. Weary of too much trying, we finally fall back upon natural geography and talk, half angrily at times, about paths and journeys and quests, about states of being and realms, the City of God, Paradise and the garden of beginning, the wonderland on the side of the mirror, the land of Narnia, and Tolkein's mountain. The list is endless. But it is all geography, all the vocabulary and symbolic reductions of geography, and all of the reductions as perfectly accurate as they are inadequate; yet we can do no better.

So the sacred then is, for us in our limitations, a world apart, a living place in the body of living that is both the containing and the contained. It is a garden, well tended and dew cleansed. Or it is the cleared and sun-warmed piazza of an alabaster palace. Or it is a fecund, calm jungle with bowered paths and still pools; or the secrecy of a favored copse filled with the half-light of cool, moist greens and the dark crevices of shadow. But always—whatever the image of the heart's moment—always the sacred is a place of strange community where what communes lacks body but exists and is perceived as personed, the whole sweetness of its communion being as nondiscursive as music and as understandable.

The sacred is an essence perceived as a place wherein all that can be grasped is equally present, where the good and the evil have changed to the warm and the cold, and neither is better; a place where light and its absence are the emotions. It is a place where we know ourselves as hollow, open-ended tubes whose hollowness too is as it must be, just as surely as the separate flutes of a pipe must likewise be unknowing and ungrasping of themselves; a place of commonality, for commonality is and is only outside of time; a place of restful abandonment, for no struggle is valid save that which lies beyond the will and can be neither advanced nor avoided by means of the will; a place of the ordinary and of the very old, both forever fixed in the vitality and sanctity of their own agedness and domestic mundanity. The sacred is, in other words, home.

But just as the Buddhist koan reminds us that the eye can never see itself, so home is that which we cannot perceive so long as we remain a part of it. "Home," like the sacred, is a locative understanding born of severance and only viewable through the yearning lens of loss. The child has home and does not know it; the adult does not have home and constantly knows it. Who can say which is better? Both circumstances are inevitable in our sense of home and so too in our discovering of the sacred.

—*Re-Discovering the Sacred*, 13–15

* * *

ADMISSION TO THE SACRED PRESUPPOSES REVERENCE

Whether the sacred is seen theistically or nontheistically and whether it is approached ecstatically or cerebrally makes no difference to that one immutable principle with which we began: Admission to the sacred presupposes reverence. And like that to which it serves as bodyguard and lover, reverence too can be effected theistically or nontheistically, ecstatically or cerebrally, or as is the case among us now, on a sliding scale that mixes and matches a little of all of them into its own means of exercise. The only thing that seems to matter is that each of us should find the form or forms of reverence from which we can construct our own trail of bread crumbs into the forest clearing with its comforting community, its beautiful lady, its serene mystery, and its terrible possibilities.

Reverence is the intercourse of life with life, the consummate art of union with the obliterating constant. Both an attitude and an action, reverence becomes in time a being, a state of whole and quiet knowing, and an enjoying of the bounds of creatureness.

Reverence is the peace of bowing to that which is so other-than-oneself as to encompass the self, so beyond form and handle that bowing is no diminishment, only fulfillment. It is acceptance of the immutable with an acceptance that releases, almost as if the restricting milkweed pod were broken at last and its million tiny selves were broadcast like angels in the rupture.

Reverence is an understanding of order and an embracing of it. It is the taking up with grace of one's inescapable place in the process of life. It is walking in balance.

Reverence is not only the walking, however, but also the template that allows one to accomplish the walking. Or put more humbly, it is a pair of spectacles through which one sees the fixed worthiness of the physical world and the appointed grandeur of the nonphysical one and is empowered thereby to participate in both of them appropriately.

Reverence is trust that informs the every gesture and decision of any life that feels it and that finds expression for itself in every controlled act; for reverence ultimately is control and a means given for self-control, just as love itself controls and self-controls. But reverence is not love; it is a cooler force, not an emotion, and lacks love's passion.

Reverence is the well-trafficked highway in and out of process, in and out of the center, in and out of the sacred's grove. Like any ancient and well-traveled highway between two capitals, reverence can be mapped. It has its laws and principles and restrictions, just as surely as it has its destinations; and it requires its own particular forms of maintenance to the point even of having, like every necessary road, its own maintenance crews and verge keepers.

But while the road holds constant, its principles and laws stable and fixed, the variable with reverence as with any road is in its travelers—in their vehicles, in their reasons for travel and their expectations of it, in their vision of the route as they move along it, and, most distinguishing, in their selective choices of what to pack for the journey and later of what to remember and record and assimilate from the journey once they have set out upon it.

Richness of experience for one traveler may be poverty for another, or an equal degree of lavishness of experience may be created for two different travelers out of very dissimilar accommodations and agenda. Bearing in mind this cordial generosity within travel, any traveler would be wise, or so it would seem, to look briefly at the constant before he or she begins to consider the variables. He or she would be well advised, in other words, to look first at reverence, the road.

—*Re-Discovering the Sacred*, 84–86

* * *

The following essay represents the long-form way that Tickle explored issues of deep importance to a meaningful Christian life in the 1980s, from her perspective of living close to the land.

Don't be surprised to encounter a sentence such as "I sliced and packaged liver while Sesame Street *emanated from the family room and Laura washed blood off the back door." —You'll see why, by the time you reach essay's end.*

THE DAY OF SLAUGHTER

Several years ago some parenting expert, probably Dr. Spock for all I know, amazed the nation by contending that one teaches one's children about sex by what one does, not by what one says. The same may also be said of religion, of course, though the truism, when applied to God, is less newsworthy by virtue of being less sensational. I discovered it, nonetheless, at the hands of another physician—my husband.

Originally it was a very simple thing, as most things are in their beginnings. It was the end of the first full calendar year of our being on the farm. Eighteen months, in other words, since we had come back to the busyness of garden produce and animal care. John was eight and a half by now and just beginning to understand that all this glory had to be paid for with the sweat of someone's brow. For the past year and a half, the sweat had come from his father's brow. Now some of it was beginning to come from his, and he was not sure he liked the change in our modus operandi too much.

Sam thought the time had come to return some of the excitement and novelty of the early days to John's life. Besides, the calves that he had bought almost two years before were now full-grown and ready to butcher. Once he had slaughtered our first beef, he said, we could truly say that we were self-sufficient on the land. Since that had been his goal all along. I was not sure how much of his motivation was John's well-being and how much was agrarian ambition. But it was a moot question, for we were going to slaughter a beef.

He and John roped Oscar, the most unlikely steer I have ever seen before or since (but one of the most delicious, I must add, though I could never understand how Sam knew that before the fact). Well, anyway, together they got a rope on Oscar and led him unprotesting to the stall in the barn which John had prepared for him. There, like an inmate on death row, Oscar had been enjoying the fat of the corn crib for almost a month.

The week after Christmas that year turned out to be the perfect one for Sam's purposes. The younger children were out of school, of course; his medical duties were light because no one who can help it gets sick over the holidays; and, to make things even more perfect, Mary was home from college. As if to add a final touch of sanction, the weather turned sharply cold on Monday afternoon—the kind of cold that lays a hard freeze on everything and doesn't let go, even in the middle of broad daylight.

On Wednesday afternoon when he came home from a short day at the office, Sam turned on the weather station and listened intently. Before dinner he watched the forecast on the television news. At supper he made his announcement. The weather was going to hold, and tomorrow we were going to butcher. A buzz of excitement went around the table with the hot biscuits. Kill a cow! How neat! Only Mary looked a bit anxious.

She was in her second year at the University of Maine. Because of the time and expense of traveling back and forth to Orono, she had spent all her holidays except Christmases with her roommates and friends—on their farms! She knew, she told me as we washed the dishes, that it was definitely time to worry.

She obviously had not spent her northern holidays in vain or conveyed her sympathies to me out of ignorance. Before I got up the next morning, she was already in the kitchen collecting all the big pots, scalding the meat grinder, covering the big table in newspaper and oilcloth, sharpening knives. She had been there.

Laura was horrified. "In here? He's going to cut it up in here?"

"We'll freeze to death out there. If you want to have any hands left, you'd better hope we do it in here."

"We! What's with this 'we' stuff? I don't intend to make hamburger this afternoon out of some steer who's eating his breakfast this morning."

"Great!" Mary was always a schemer, and I was beginning to get her drift, the reason for her early and portentous arranging of the utensils. "Then you can babysit Rebecca and Sam junior and also cook supper, while Mama and I do this." Neat kid, that girl. Crafty, but a good one to have on your side.

Laura gave it some consideration. Being bright, she knew she'd been outmaneuvered. The question was simply whether or not she minded. Since everyone was going to end up dog tired before the day was over anyway, and since she would infinitely rather watch kids and make sandwiches than grind meat and freeze roasts, the only real loss was to her ego. She apparently decided against protesting and went instead to start on the beds.

Mary's predictions of the day were as accurate as her preparations had been. She and Sam took John with them as they went trudging off to the barn and the waiting Oscar. Rebecca observed for what was to be the first of many times that day that she really didn't think it was fair for John to go and her to not. "Later, Princess," was Sam's response to her as he shut the back door behind them.

Within five minutes I heard the shot, but no one else seemed to notice until John came popping like Father Christmas into the back door, eyes big and cheeks rosy. "Golly, Mom, he just dropped him right there in the stall. You shoulda seen how he did it. Dumb cow didn't know what happened. He and Mary are hoisting him up now. I gotta go watch 'em gut him," and he was gone again.

"Gag!" said Laura from behind me. "Don't men ever get tired of killing things?"

"I'm not sure this qualifies as killing things. We intend to eat him, you know."

"Sure it qualifies. It's just justified, is all. They're still getting the same bang out of it. Just look at that kid. He's excited to death because he got to see a cow shot."

"I still don't think it's fair that John gets to go," Rebecca butted in.

"Hush, baby," Laura Lee said absently, already paying little or no attention to Becca's complaint, and she set off toward the basement to start a load of laundry. "Well, I don't," was all I heard from Rebecca's retreating back as she docilely followed, leaving a trail of underwear and bath towels behind her.

The next hour was punctuated by John's enthusiastic messages from the back door, messages that always began, "Mom! Mom!" until I could get to the back door to receive the latest piece of intelligence.

"Mom, did you know Oscar made this big, huge cloud of steam when Dad cut him open?"

"Yes, son, I knew that."

"Wow!" and the door slammed shut again leaving me unsure of what had wowed him—the event or my information base.

"Mom! Mom!"

"Yes, John."

"Dad says I can have the horns if you say so and I saw 'em off."

"Right, son, but I think your brother may not like it."

"He's not out there working like I am. Fair's fair."

And then, reluctantly, "Mom! Dad says for me to bring Sam out for a little while. He wants to show us how the heart valves work, but he says it's too cold for Rebecca."

After the anatomy lesson was over (and I have to be honest and say that no child from here has ever failed an anatomy test, especially not one on the heart, lungs, or liver—a fact which is due, I am sure, directly to Sam's insistence on showing them at every slaughter exactly where muscles insert and blood vessels run and cusps shut), we progressed naturally, if not easily, into the business of the day and half the night.

The brains came in the door for Daddy's supper. I can't stand the things and never could when my own father loved them. The liver was ushered in steaming by a disgruntled Mary, who opened the back door and hollered to no one in particular, "Take this thing!" and was gone again. I sliced and packaged liver while *Sesame Street* emanated from the family room and Laura washed blood off the back door.

"That's a waste of time if I ever saw one," I told her, but she was determined.

We had both finished before the first quarters hit the kitchen, carried this time by both Daddy and Mary, an ecstatic John tagging behind them. Sam moves swiftly when he's working and there was considerable grace in his cuts as he portioned and severed, sawed and boned. By four o'clock the quarters were rendered into steaks, roasts, and other. The other was going to take five more hours to be rendered into stew meat and hamburger.

Laura had been relegated to a very small but bloodless end of the kitchen from which she had faithfully been dispensing sandwiches and drinks for three hours already. Mary, with the bulk of the barn work done, sat down to begin the grinding; and I went on wrapping, marking, and freezing. We didn't see Sam again for a couple of hours except when he brought the ribs in to be severed and parceled. By dusk, however, he had finished the outside cleanup, washed the hide and put it in the tanning solution, and fed the stock. He came in the back door with the last of the pots for Laura to wash in the kitchen sink.

"Where's Becca?" he said.

"Pouting downstairs because she never even got to go out."

"Becca! Becca!" he called down the steps.

"What?" came an almost petulant, almost-five-years-old answer.

"Come see what I brought you from the barn," and he pulled a whitish looking piece of something from his pocket. He got instant attention from the whole kitchen as well as from the family room.

Ever the showman, he insisted on waiting until Becca was upstairs before he took string out of the kitchen drawer and would it tightly around one end of the flesh thing in his hand. Then, grinning—and so were Mary and I by now—he opened the bean sack and took out, very deliberately, three dried beans and dropped them into the other and open end of the thing in his hand. Sitting down in his accustomed chair and with Becca practically in his lap, he put the open end of the thing to his lips and began to blow. It expanded before her eyes, and they expanded before all of us. "What is it, Daddy? What is it? What is it?" over and over again, her insistence growing in direct proportion to Sam's unwillingness to quit blowing and talk.

Finally, when the thing had got as big as a basketball, Sam quit. He took it from his mouth, twisted the end and tied it as one ties a balloon. Handing it to her, he said, "Now feel it but be real easy with it until it dries." She did. He showed her how to rattle it and make the beans roll around merrily in it. "Now," he said after a few minutes of play, "we're going to hang it up here on this nail over the counter so it can dry. By tomorrow it will have turned almost clear and you can play with it." She was enthralled.

"But what is it?" said Laura.

"Oscar's bladder," Mary answered.

"His what?"

"His bladder," Mary repeated, plainly enjoying herself as much as Sam was.

"I had one every winter when I was little," he offered. "It was my favorite plaything."

"Oh, God!" said Laura.

But Rebecca was unmoved by it all as she pulled a chair over and began to gently bat the bladder back and forth on its nail.

With much less ado but with just as delighted a result, Sam took from his pocket four cleaned-out hooves, and Sam junior was quick to get the message. Now they each had a fair share of the day's goodies and each was content except for Rebecca's halfhearted protests that it was no fair the boys could take their parts to bed with them and hers had to stay hung up over the kitchen counter. Basically, however, she was too tired to really care and Laura was too disgusted to give her much slack. So the young ones were bedded down finally, and the old ones sat up till almost midnight grinding. The day was done and we were "self-sufficient on the land" at last.

As a sequence of events, we would repeat the process many times before we got to be few enough and old enough to no longer need to kill our own beef. The boys, during those years, took turns over who got the horns and who got the hooves, but Becca always ended up with the bladder.

The horns and hooves would turn up from time to time in various interesting and arresting uses. They were turned into the predictable powder horns and carved into the predictable boxes and handles. One year the best jack-o'-lantern we ever had sported a pair of somebody's horns above a mean, Brunhilde kind of face. But the bladder always stayed hung on the nail above the kitchen counter when it was not being played with. Though it changed from year to year and sometimes broke before its replacement arrived, it was the only ball in our history that was always faithfully returned to its place after every use.

Our friends and intimates got used to seeing it there, just as they probably got used to jack-o'-lanterns with real horns. Most of the adults, in fact, would take it down and play with it themselves as they stood in the kitchen talking and visiting while I cooked our meal or cleaned up one we had just shared. By the very nature of things, of course, most of those familiar friends were writers or editors or publishers, folks who could accept a cow's bladder with more grace than most. One in particular, however, was important to me.

She was a longtime and dear friend, almost fifteen years my junior and still at the start of her career the first time she pulled the bladder off its nail, and asked, "What's this?"

"Oscar's bladder," Rebecca answered.

"I thought so. I haven't had one in years," Lynne responded, turning it over to make the beans roll and rattle.

The next time she came to visit, it was Covenant's bladder hanging on the nail and she rolled it in her hands more thoughtfully than she had the previous one.

"What's up?" I asked her.

"The boys do anything bizarre with Covenant's horns and hooves?"

"No, they had to split the hooves this year because Covic didn't have horns."

"Oh." She was still propped against the counter, moving the ball in her hands and thinking.

"Penny for your thoughts."

"Not worth a penny," she said. "At least not yet."

"What're you working on?"

"A piece I really want to do—have ever since I picked up Oscar's bladder last winter—on death. I see it everywhere I go in town. And when I'm on the road! Lord, you wouldn't believe the number of dead animals you see in the middle of the road these days!" She shook her head as if to clear what was in it. Then she tried again. "When I'm out here, it seems so easy. The kids are so unconcerned with it. They play with bladders and hooves and horns and eat meat and pluck chickens and watch Sam shoot coons and it doesn't bother any of you."

"Come on, you grew up this way. You remember how it is on a farm. There's always more life than the land can support!" I was a little disconcerted, I suppose, by the unexpected direction our evening was taking. "You kill part of it to eat. You kill part of it to keep it from killing you, literally or figuratively. Nature kills the rest, either before or after it reproduces itself. We're built on death here or anywhere else. There's just no concrete or pretense out here to hide it."

"Only a Christian could say that," she responded.

"Say what?"

"Say we're built on death."

"No," I said, "any realist could say that. And any religious man could say that we should value the death we're built on. And any moralist could say that there's a difference in sentient death and non-sentient, with human obligation falling on us to relieve the former rather than the latter, and so forth and so on." I was disgusted, faintly but definitely, by this brand of quasi-effeteness, especially in a woman who was neither an intellectual dullard nor an emotional patsy.

"And what would any Christian say?" she pushed on, ignoring my testiness.

"Beats me," I said finally, being unable, much to my chagrin, to come up with even the feeblest answer to her question.

"Maybe I'll ask Sam why he thinks it's important to give the kids these things every time he butchers." She was ruminating more to herself than to me, and I forgot about the conversation until two nights later.

It was her last night with us on this visit before going back to her apartment in the big city and her next assignment. We were in the kitchen again, just after supper, and I was still loading the dishwasher when she took down the ball and began to rotate it in her two hands.

"Did you ask Sam?"

"Yeah," she grinned.

"Well," I said. "What did he say?"

"What I should have known without asking."

"Which was . . . ?"

"Which was that he gives the stuff to them so they can have fun."

"That's all?"

"No. He also said he gives it to them so they won't take themselves too seriously."

Well, she was right about one thing. I can't say that about just any Christian, but both of us certainly should have known what mine would say.

—*The Tickle Papers,* chapter 4

* * *

Only one who lives deliberately as a part of the natural world and its needs could write this short essay in which living and dying are intimately connected. The quiet yet strong, spiritual yet rebellious voice is palpable.

TO MY PEAR TREES

After my bath I stay long in the tub, listening to the soft, cotton suck of the water as it circles the drain. I lie through that instant of near bursting when my bones take up the weight of my flesh again from the retreating water. I feel the vacuum as it pulls my back hard against the porcelain bottom and as flat as if I were young again. My skin and hair release the water, droplet by droplet, to the gravity of air and drain, and I live briefly in the slow effervescence of their drying.

Even when it's finally gone, this will still be my water. It will come back again to me, to my body, to our house. It leaves now in copper pipes which run off into cool clay ones which, in turn, drain just beyond the orchard fence into the gravel overrun where, purified, it sinks slowly under the roots of grass, trees, and vines.

Some spring soon it will flower or make milk for a new calf; some fall soon it will drop from the juice of our pears or fatten a steer for market. This water leaves us only for a few seasons.

In its origin it is not our water, of course. City water was brought into this part of the country years ago, brought without the consent of those who farm here, brought in the name of the public good, and paid for by assessment of the unwilling. Our house, like the others in the community, had always been plumbed into its own well. When the water came, each well, ours included, had to be disconnected—severed from itself—and the houses reconnected to pipes whose name no one knew. In our homes water had become a manufactured necessity, a commodity to be produced elsewhere and transported at great expense to a dependent market.

The outside water was different. The water in the barn, the water in the hen house, the water in the hose pipes—that was our water—ours from our well and brought up by our pump. The houses may have had to be connected to utility pipes, but not the farms themselves. On the days when the utility company had the water shut off to repair the lines or even on the days when the pressure in the inside faucets was low, we could still trip the pump switch and draw up what was ours, what was not another's to shut off or treat or pollute. It was an independence that even the younger children, despite their hatred of summer watering chores, fiercely valued.

Like me, they remembered the hot days in past summers when the well went out; when we watched anxiously as their father climbed up and down, up and down, from the ground to the well-house roof, rigging a homemade derrick; when in that devastating heat of 105 degrees, he pulled the well-shaft by hand, inch after inch, until it stood a hundred feet above us like a prayer tower into the belly of heaven. They remembered, too, the afternoon when, a new valve in place, he sank the shaft back into the water table; how we all stood waiting in the heat while he primed and primed and the water came racing out to the frantic fields and thirsty garden; how I cried when we saw it come; how he slapped the children on the backs; how we had an early supper and an early bedtime; and how the water sang all night in the hose pipes.

It was not long after that that the machines came. They were a mile or so away from us, near the village; parked for a day or two, growing in number until there were seven of them—backhoes and Cats and two flatbeds of concrete pipe. On Thursday of the last week of September the stacks of ten-inch pipe were dropped, a dozen pipes per strapped bundle set out every thirty or forty feet along the roadside. On Saturday the crews came and began the digging. Backhoes along the edges of the road, backhoes into yards, backhoes crisscrossing the roadbed. It was suddenly two miles to get around them, two extra miles around the crisscrossing to the school and community center, two extra miles to the market where we sold our eggs. Sewers were coming! Once more, without having been asked or even told, we stood helplessly as the heavy equipment lumbered across the land. The water we now had to pay to have hauled in was about to be wasted, hauled away, and we would have to pay for that, too. Our water was soon to pass totally through and beneath us in a sealed system of delivery as if it were a product and not a given.

The rains of October came, and the machines bogged down in the mud. We rejoiced when the great crustaceans were hauled away. All winter we hoped they would not come back to work the ditches. Of course they did, but times were hard, and there were fewer men, fewer machines. Only a dozen houses or so lost their last hold on the cycle of nature that had, since the beginning, nurtured them. As the fall ended and the winter began to move in, the machines were taken early to storage. They will come again next month or the one after that; eventually they will get us like they have gotten everyone else. So I lie long in this tub, feeling the water leave and sending it with love to my pear trees. How else, in what other way, can one mourn for the death of water, if indeed it is the water that is dying?

—*The Graces We Remember,* chapter 3

* * *

A poem written for her infant son. Death is only tragic when it is a surprise—and we will never understand it.

For Wade

May 29—June 11, 1971

There was such an easiness in your going,
such a stilling peace for us once they said,
"He's gone."
It filled up all our days that came and went
until our friends began to say:
"Won't you come to dinner?
"Attend this play?
"See ballet?
"Take for your sorrow some cliché of
'God will provide' or
'Life must go on'?"

And so it is, my son,
that the work of your burying
has begun.

—*Selections*

* * *

This is taken from a collection of essays and personal stories about Advent and Christmas.

NAME THIS CHILD

I was seventeen years old when I was first introduced to the psychology of names. Away from home for the first time, I was attending one of those small, southern women's colleges that were long on academic excellence and short on hard cash. The faculty, in those days before equal opportunity legislation, was composed primarily of independently wealthy and brilliantly educated females. One of them was Francesca Boas, daughter of Franz Boas, the father of American anthropology. She fascinated me (and every other undergraduate), and I dogged her heels incessantly.

It must have been October or early November when she laid on me the gem about names. Primitive peoples, she said, even some nonprimitive peoples living in the midst of civilized societies, regard an individual's name as containing the essence of his or her personness. She laid it out before me almost nonchalantly and then watched while a whole system of contradictions and curiosities began to make sense to me: the injunction against taking the Lord's name in vain, the business of christening under a saint's name, the use of Jehovah instead of the sacrosanct Yahweh, the giving of titles and surrogates.

Like every other piece of information that explains some part of human experience, I found this one to be enormously satisfying. . . . That early freshman wonder never entirely lost its glow, but it subsided eventually, becoming one of those insights that was integrated but never was foremost in my thoughts again until years later when we moved to the country.

A thousand things to name! Like Adam walking into the Garden, the children spent hours naming cats and dogs and cows and chickens. Each new species had to be individually enfranchised as Sam brought it in and added it to the farm's growing population.

Much to our surprise, the whole process was conducted with remarkable care. The new cow that would rather be rubbed and stroked than fed was named, affectionately, Silly Sally. The new Gertrudis with horns was named Saint because she looked like the winged ox that is the icon for St. Luke. The bull was immediately named Bull with a capital B since by common agreement that's what he was. By much the same process, Big Mama was christened Big Mama. Nothing else could possibly have covered all her virtues: her broad posterior, her cud-chewing deliberateness, her soft white hide, her gentle slow eyes, and her easy affection. She lived out her days with us and annually confirmed the children's accuracy by consistently presenting us with the finest calf of the year.

So we settled in on the Lucy Goosey Farm (a terrible name, but the children's by unanimous vote). . . . In time, all of the above tended to reproduce according to the species and place in life assigned to each. . . .

Mary was named Mary because she was born to Big Mama on the morning of the day in 1979 when big sister Mary, much loved and highly valued by the younger children for her unending indulgences, was to come home from college for the spring holiday. Oscar was named Oscar because he had incredibly round ears, walked all his life with a wobble, and looked like an idiot, even for a cow. Beauregard was Molly's calf, and two weeks after calving, Molly was the first of the herd to die. But Beauregard was so elegant, so delicate of foot, so careful of his deportment that only the stars knew he was an orphan. Mary (sister, that is) and the younger children bottle-fed him all summer until he could make it alone, but even in that indignity he remained a dandy, demanding that his lip be wiped and his coat stroked clean after each feeding. Only Beauregard would have fit him.

Two years later and in a meadow full of cows, Oscar still was wobbling. He still looked like a bovine idiot the day we penned him up to fatten. For the whole next summer and fall after we had slaughtered, butchered, and frozen him, the children would laugh and giggle at supper. It was always, "Please pass Oscar," instead of "Please pass the meatloaf" or the roast or whatever. The memory of that pathetic dottiness was so pervasive as to even survive metamorphosis.

But in time I began to remark on more than the humor in all of this. For instance, Mary grew to be beautiful—not a pretty cow, although she was—but beautiful. Her eyelashes were the thickest I have ever seen on any cow, and her coat was much whiter than her mother's despite the fact that she had been sired by Bull, who was black as coal. She was hardly more than a calf herself when she began to indulge the younger children, and they even rode her once or twice before I made them stop for her sake. She always got special hay from them and the treats of apples and pears, and even turnips in the later months. It was as if she and they both grew into her name. . . .

It was then that I remembered Francesca again and perceived a corollary to her principle. All things grow into their name, agreed; and all things likewise grow into the names they have given, named and namers reinforcing each other, creating each other for every day of life itself and long beyond the death of the body.

We still see Oscar from time to time in somebody else's dumb steer. For years after Oscar was gone, the children would "pass Oscar" on nights when the meat was tough, and I was supposed to understand, thereby, that the cook had failed for at least that meal. And Francesca, herself long since dead, must have smiled one day when the grandson who wasn't even born when Oscar grazed our fields asked me to please cook him some Oscar for supper.

Mary died in 1982 as gently as she had lived, a calf half-grown within her. The children mourned her as sincerely as if she had been a part of them, for of all the herd, she indeed was knitted to them across all lines and boundaries by a name and by a resulting pattern of life. One day I listened with a kind of quiet joy as John explained to Rebecca that he was going out beyond Mary's Hill to target practice and that she wasn't to follow him. So they had named among themselves the spot where she finally lay down to go.

What is New Year's Day for the world at large is also the Feast of the Holy Name for the church, the day that marks the circumcision of the Christ child. . . . Before the day is done, I still walk out by myself to Mary's Hill for a little while and think there about what it means to know the name of God and to be yourself called by it.

—*What the Land Already Knows,* chapter 9

* * *

Last, a short reflection pulled from the introductory remarks in Tickle's last book about the sayings and teachings of Jesus—included in this section because of how it represents her way of writing about faith with wonder, rather than any sense of conclusion. It reads like a prose poem.

HUMAN LIFE CANNOT END

What [the teachings of Jesus in the Gospels] share and rest on is the very simple principle that human life cannot end. Once we are born, we are. Always. Without end or hope of end, we are. Life is eternal; death is eternal. In life or in death, we are without hope of cessation. And if that is not a terrifying thought, I hope never to hear one.

—*The Words of Jesus,* 30

2

Stories and Sins

An Easter Apology to My Guineas

Today I boiled your children.
I never thought of cooking
as anything
but love
until I saw the eggs
drowning in my pot
and was amazed
by the magnitude
of your loss.

—*Selections*

* * *

This chapter includes portions of essays written for magazines, a commencement address Tickle gave just after 9/11, very personal reflections on the importance of the stories of faith and the importance of death and loss, poems, and selections from Greed. *Also included here is the complete text of one of her best-selling, most important, and least-known works to twenty-first-century readers: the short fiction* The Story of Two Johns.

The scope of Tickle's religious storytelling is always wide and varied in terms of religious and spiritual traditions considered, and both objectively and subjectively understood.

PAGANS AND PATRIARCHS

Welcome to summer. Officially and totally summer in the Northern Hemisphere. It's certifiably summer by every means of our accounting, be it psychological or physical, historical or theological. Which of these we choose to employ makes no difference. This is still Summer, with a capital "S."

Experientially, spring began to morph into summer weeks ago for most of us, but astrologically or geologically speaking, that transfer was not complete until last Friday—last Friday at 7:59 p.m. EDT . . . the Summer Solstice—that night which, for our ancient forebears, was the most mysterious of the year.

Before the Christianization of Europe, the mystery was seen as the death of the Oak King and the advent of the Holly King. It was the slip or rift in time when the Earth began to bear down in birth to deliver her bounty. It was the interruption of the ordinary through which the spirits, dressed in new foliage, danced in the moonlight to the devils' tunes. *Litha*, they called it, and *Litha* it still is for Wiccans and Neo-pagans. And *Litha* the whole season will be for them until *Mabon*—that comes this year just as precisely and on point as *Litha* did—except in September, not June . . . for [September] is the time of the Autumnal Equinox.

While physicists and astronomers may speak in the patois of the sciences and while Wiccans may speak in the hoary vernacular of their heritage, most of us in this hemisphere speak either not at all, or almost not at all, about the strange slippage of spring into summer. Those of us who live in the country, as I and my family do, still mark the seasons, but not so often the sky. Our view is more horizontal than that these days, and our physical world considerably less God-haunted. But liturgy, of whatever origin or persuasion, has always given form and formality to what the body knows and cannot otherwise convey to the mind. Such is the function of liturgy, in fact, be it Christian or otherwise.

In the case of Christianity, which is the tradition in which my own faith is implacably rooted, and in the case of the liturgy which gives it form, our secularly un-remarked-upon passage away from spring is still very much remarked upon during the first full week of summer. That means that twice this week, Christians will stop and consider, hopefully to our souls' benefit, the stories of two men. One of them biblical, the other not. The biblical saint is so well known as to need no great mention here. That is, on Tuesday, the 24th, Christians will say prayers of thanks for the life of John the Baptizer, herald and forerunner of Our Lord. And on Saturday the 28th, we will give thanks for Irenaeus, Bishop of Lyons.

Now, most of us, whether Christian or simply Christianized, secular or other, to some greater or lesser extent, have a sense of who John the Baptizer was. Irenaeus, on the other hand, is a bit of a stretch. Irenaeus lived in the second century, dying in old age at some point near or just before 200 CE. He was, as his citation indicates, bishop of Lyons, the second one for that city ever to have, in fact. The whole idea of "Church" was that new in the mid and late decades of the second century. Yet it was that very newness of institutionalization that makes Irenaeus so important, so worthy of being the nonbiblical saint with whom summer opens. Irenaeus, you see, was a disciple of Polycarp; and Polycarp had been a disciple of St. John the Evangelist and Gospeler. That is to say, Irenaeus knew intimately the man who had known intimately the man who had known intimately Jesus of Nazareth. And what Irenaeus learned from Polycarp and, through him, from Polycarp's own mentor, was sufficient. It was sufficient for Irenaeus to stand against the persecutions of the emperor Marcus Aurelius from 161–180 CE, and it was sufficient for him to become the first theologian of that tenuous entity that was becoming the Church. It was sufficient, as well, for him to be the first Christian to argue for the four Gospels of Matthew, Mark, Luke, and John as authoritative and, more than that, as their being the only authoritative ones.

When Christians speak of the canonical Jesus, they can speak because of Irenaeus. And conversations about the historical Jesus or the theoretical Jesus or the edited Jesus or whatever other way one may choose for arriving at a distant Jesus always, eventually, trip over old Irenaeus. There he stands, haloed by the centuries right smack at the beginning of summer and saying, "This. This is what I heard from the man who knew the man who saw and heard and recorded it." All of which is a sobering way to enter, God-haunted, into summer.

So be it.

originally published on Jim Wallis's "God's Politics" blog, *Sojourners*, June 22, 2008

* * *

The first selection in what comes next is fiction with autobiographical overtones, originally published as a (quite successful) picture book. Following it is a true story about Tickle's eldest son, John, written upon the occasion of his going off to college, from the final chapter in The Tickle Papers.

THE STORY OF TWO JOHNS

[Fiction]

Before he moved to town, my grandfather, whose name was John, lived in the country and raised pigs and timber and cotton and children—lots of children.

He fought in the War Between the States on the side of the South and he used to say that he had lain, hurt and dying, for three days on the battlefield of Shiloh before the medics could even treat his wounds.

Grandfather believed in schools, in going to church, and in little girls—especially in little girls—and I have loved him dearly from as long ago as I can remember.

Every summer, when I was a little girl, we would go to Grandfather's house to visit. Grandfather was never there and was always everywhere all at the same time. It used to confuse me terribly, but when I was little, adults almost always confused me anyway. But there was one thing I was certain of—I was certain that Grandpa loved me. I could feel him loving me in every room of that house.

When we were visiting, I always slept in Grandpa's room.

In the afternoons when it was too hot for me to take a nap, I would lie on Grandpa's big, high bed and make up stories about him and Grandmother. There were pictures of him everywhere in that room. One framed on Grandmother's dresser and two stuck around the edge of her bureau mirror and, on the far wall, a big picture of him in uniform.

But the picture that I love most to remember was the one that hung just over the doorway to the hall. I could see it from the bed and from up there Grandpa could look right back down at me on the bed.

It looked just like Grandpa. He had on his best grey suit with the high-cut vest and his watch chain showed just below his beard—his wonderful, wonderful beard. It was long and white and curly and it tickled you if you got too close. And it quivered all the way down to his buttons when he got mad at you. When Grandfather got mad, you always knew it by that beard. And his eyes were as blue as glass—fierce blue eyes that laughed and loved you and were always clear even when he was an old man.

When I was little, I loved Grandpa's house almost as much as I loved Grandpa. He and I used to share secrets about that house, about the deep cedar closets where Grandma stored her quilts for the summer—and about the dark spaces between the walls where only children could hide and play—about the old trunks and tins and furniture that were stacked up in the outside sheds—and about the cool, damp earth under the house where no other adults ever wanted to go. I went in all those places and never alone. I could have stayed forever under the house on Grandfather's farm, but instead we always had to go back home.

Every November, when the weather began to turn cold, my father would say, "We'll go home this year for Christmas," and I knew that I would soon be back in Grandpa's big, high bed watching him watch me from his place above the door.

At Christmastime it was always cold in the bedrooms. The old painted lanterns were too smoked to give much light and the grownups would always gossip late around the frontroom stove. When I was put to bed, I would wiggle down under the covers of Grandpa's bed and tell him stories about all the things I had done since the last July.

I knew most of Grandfather's stories by heart. My father had told me all of them himself. I knew all about Shiloh and General Forrest and Bull Run. I knew how, before supper every night, Grandpa used to chew the edge of his lower lip and look across the fields with those fierce blue eyes of his until he had planned the next day's work.

I knew from my father just how Grandfather had carved his big, high bed with his own hands and given it to Grandma on their wedding day. Every time I looked out from under the covers I could see Grandfather's hands turning the spindles with his knife.

I knew, without looking, that out the window and almost hidden in the snow was the schoolhouse Grandfather had helped to build because Grandfather was a believing man who heard your lessons and asked you spelling every night after supper and before you went to bed.

Sometimes, on the nights before Christmas, my father would sit beside me on Grandpa's bed and tell me stories about his boyhood on the farm and about what Grandfather had been like as a young man. I knew from him how Grandfather's sword felt in your hand long before I was ever allowed to hold it myself. I understood how proud Grandfather was of having been a captain under General Lee long before I was tall enough to see the pictures on Grandmother's bureau.

Father said that Grandfather always stood like a soldier even after there was no war left to fight. And he ran that house like a good general runs an army. His boots were clean and his riding crop was sharp. He was a good and gentle man who loved little girls and hunting dogs and the tawny color of the gold coins he always carried in his pocket. My father used to tell me so in the dark at night.

My father always said I was just like Grandfather even if I was a girl. Every time I would chew the edge of my lower lip, my father would say, "Just like Papa," and I would love to hear him say it.

I would take out one of the gold coins that Grandpa had left for me to have as my very own and hold it tight and wish that I could grow up to be just like him. I would practice looking fierce and wish with all my heart that my eyes were blue and I could grow a beard.

I would sit in church on Sundays and try to understand all the things that Grandpa knew. I learned my spelling and made my father hear me say it because I knew that was what Grandfather thought all good children should do.

But that was all a long, long time ago, of course, and I love Grandpa even more now than I did then because I have grown up. Also, I have a little boy of my own now who has fierce blue eyes as clear as glass, and his name is John, too, just like Grandpa's.

Young John sits on the back steps of my house in the late afternoons and stares at the trees in the backyard while he plans the next day's work—he won't come in to eat his supper until he's done with planning.

John swings a sword when he plays. He chews the edge of his lower lip when he is daydreaming and he pulls on his ear to think.

I never saw my grandfather face-to-face or touched his hand or felt his skin, for he had been dead a long time when I was born. I used to cry about that because when I was a very little girl, I thought it was unfair of Grandfather to be where I could not touch him.

But now in young John I see Grandpa just as he used to be—just the way he was when I saw him in my father's eyes or smiling back at me from the mirror when I was little and he was me.

I see Grandfather still in the farm he tilled and in the stones that mark his grave.

He is my grandfather and he is a believing man who looks at me from young John's fine, blue eyes and makes me know that the more we live, the more there is of him.

* * *

THE SIGN OF THE EAGLE

John is going off to college this year. At our house, as at most others, that effectively means that John is going.

He will come back, of course, in the sense that his leaving is not a severance of his roots from our soil; but he will have to think more and more each year from now on about when and how to come back. He will increasingly have to plan for the dates and means of coming back. He will have to work at us, in other words.

It is a shift in things that I have always found to be a little sad as well as a little hard because, although John doesn't know it yet, Sam and I will have to work at him more and more now. His coming will be something we have to check the dates on and arrange things for. And the conversations of his coming back will be, as they have been with Nora and Mary and Philip and Laura, active exercises in trying to reconnect when most of the pieces are missing. When experiences diverge, only the supra-structure of remembrance can cause them to converge again.

So I have spent these last few months telling John good-bye in ways he hasn't even caught me at, in all the subtle ways a mother has, in all the "Do you remembers?" that will be my touchstone in ten years when he comes back and doesn't know how to begin again.

Despite the innocence of what lies ahead and of the bridges I am so carefully building, John has been building a few of his own for future use, ones he doesn't yet understand the reasons for even as he is building them. Instinct, be it physical or spiritual, is a most wonderful thing and the freedom to follow it, without self-editing, a most wonderful gift. John has it.

John is a country boy. He would hate to hear me say that because he is also very definitely a sophisticated kid who is as comfortable in the middle of Washington or Cincinnati as he is in the middle of a pasture. But the truth remains that he can gut and butcher a deer without direction; that he can run a tractor as well as his father can; that he can drop a squirrel at two hundred yards or heave a bale of hay for five—not one of which abilities is a function of urban life, whether John likes it or not.

Even more revealing is the fact that John tolerates only two pieces of jewelry. One is his watch. It cost him almost all of his first week's pay the summer he was fifteen and went to work during the day as a gofer for a construction crew.

The watch was one he had envied on his best friend and had longed for for two whole semesters. It not only tells the usual tales of time, date, seconds, and appointments; it also has a calculator that has tended to be invaluable in algebra, and a memory that stores more facts than I would have thought an IBM could house.

You ask John now for his Social Security number and he asks his watch; his checking account number and he punches his watch; our dental insurance policy number and he raises his wrist to inquire. Things have got to such a pitch, in fact, that I am hysterical if he leaves his watch at home when we go someplace together; and it is Mama who always goes instantly to town to buy new batteries when the thing on John's wrist begins to beep that the energy in its innards is getting low.

But John's other piece of finery is almost exactly the opposite of his watch. Around his neck, on a short, heavy chain and almost always deliberately hidden under his shirt, John wears his baptismal medal. I don't know, because I didn't buy it, but I suspect that the chain is made of some kind of steel or heavy alloy. Whatever its composition, it is certainly impervious to the obvious threats of John's lifestyle. He bought the chain, just as he also paid to have the medal soldered to it, with some of his money from this summer's job as a carpenter's assistant, and he has worn it consistently ever since. The medal is intimately tied to John's leaving.

We are not, as you know, Roman Catholic at our house, but Episcopalian (or, as our bishops are fond of saying, Anglo-Catholic. It is a small point to most folks and not one I have ever been too eager to belabor publicly, although at home we have always tried to make the distinction clear to the children). As Episcopalians—or Anglo-Catholics, if you prefer—we baptize our children under their given names and not under a saint's. When, therefore, John was baptized, he was baptized as John because it was his name and his grandfather's name before him. Because it was also a liturgical name, however, he, more or less by default, assumed all the icons and churchly heritage of St. John, the Gospeler, the Apostle, the author of the Apocalypse, the beloved of Our Lord.

Such a thing is a heavy accretion to lay upon an eight-pound baby, if one thinks about it much. To be honest, I didn't. I simply accepted in his name and stored for safekeeping and his future use the gifts that he received on his christening day, including his baptismal medal.

Flat, square, and small—no more than three-quarters of an inch in any given direction—and fashioned in sterling silver, it shows the head, beak, and upper wing curvature of a ferocious, handsome, and watchful eagle. Across the lower portion of the eagle's feathered chest is a scroll that reads simply "St. John" and bears the sign of the cross beside the name. On the back, the givers, dear friends of many years' standing, had had "J.C.T. 7/11/70" engraved in an Old English script. Only this and nothing more, to quote Poe.

Afraid that as an infant he would swallow the medal or hurt himself trying, I had put it away with the rest of his keepsakes. From time to time over the years of his infancy and boyhood, I would show it to him and tell him who St. John was. As he grew older, he would sometimes ask to have something by or about

St. John as his choice for our evening story time, but he never asked about the eagle.

Like most Episcopalian kids, long after the Thanksgiving of the starlings and long before his present level of maturity, John got churched—or at least the church made a pass at trying to get his attention.

He went through weeks of instruction, which finally culminated in his confirmation and his admission to Holy Communion. How much of it took and how much has yet to take is anybody's guess and probably none of anybody's business, at least not at the moment. But he did, in the process, get introduced to symbols, including the centuries-old symbols or icons of the Evangelists—the man, the lion, the winged ox, and the eagle. That took. It took right in my kitchen, right in the middle of my canning the first of that particular spring's peaches.

"Why do you suppose folks took animals as signs for Saints Matthew, Mark, Luke, and John?" was how he began.

"I don't know. What does Father King say about it?"

"Says because symbols were safer than words when the Christians were being persecuted."

"Don't you believe that?"

"Yeah, why not? But why animals? Why not things?

"Did you ask?"

"Yeah."

"Well?" This was getting to be an exasperating conversation, and I didn't envy any priest who had to take a bunch of twelve-year-olds through the process two or three times every year of his clerical life.

"Well, he said he thought I ought to be asking why the Indians didn't use things instead of animals for their totem poles."

"Holy Toledo!" I said, not having expected so direct an answer and having burned myself on hot peach syrup as a result.

"Yeah, that's what I said," my son responded, and went off to ponder something more accessible and less dangerous.

Sometime later—I don't remember when, I just recall that it was cold outside and wintry enough so that John was in instead of out that afternoon—I asked him about the Indians.

"Appears to me," he said thoughtfully, "as if a person would probably be a lot more comfortable being a bear than a bow and arrow, 'specially since a bear can move on its own hook without having to have another Indian around."

"I'll buy that," I said.

"Except, of course," he continued without even noticing me, "that the real question is, What's so good about being a bear—other than the fact that it beats being a bow and arrow?"

"Well, I can certainly understand that," I said. End of conversation and end of my active memory of the whole until this summer when John came and asked me for his baptismal medal.

"Sure," I said, getting it out of my jewelry box and giving it to him. "But what do you want it for?"

"Oh," he said with an elaborate casualness. "I guess I just feel more like being an eagle now than I used to." The piece of fashioned silver slipped deftly into his jeans pocket. "Thanks for keeping it for me all these years," he added as he turned and left the room.

Which was last June and the end of that conversation until one day last week when John leaned over to lift a box for me and the medal fell out, as it does from time to time, from under his shirt. As he set the box in place on the shop table, he stood back, dusted his hands and unconsciously raised his right hand to drop the medal back under his T-shirt. I caught his hand as it went toward the medal.

"Want to tell me why now?" I asked.

He grinned, the dimple he used to hate and his girlfriend now adores deepened to frame his lower face. He shrugged. "I guess it's kind of like your wedding ring," he said. "Kind of a calling, the cross and the eagle and my name on there all together—kind of a calling."

Well, son, may it be a good calling, as good and as full as your father's and mine have been. May it bring you home from time to time and, more important, may it carry you far away again. May it teach you praise and cause you to worship, and may it, in the end, also be a holy vocation.

* * *

Here is a poignant essay about serious personal loss in Tickle's life—"At two weeks of age, our second son and fifth child died of pneumonia."—and the power of both inherited and acquired faith to help in understanding it. Rereading this now, I am reminded of a few lines from Faulkner's short story "The Bear": "Be scared. You can't help that. But don't be afraid."[6]

PATRON SAINTS AND A STORY OF GRIEF

I was named for my father, whose given name was Philip. Had I belonged to a Catholic family, I doubtless would have claimed St. Philip as my patron saint. As it was, my limited exposure to the saint occurred in the years of my early schooling during and just after the Second World War, when we children were required to read, from time to time, sections of Butler's *Lives of the Saints* for our literature or social studies classes. It was an assignment I always stoutly refused to honor. My Methodist-born father was deathly afraid of "all things papist," as he so charmingly put it, and I was deathly afraid of reading about things that were physically painful. Between the two of us, therefore, we managed to find more than enough reason for me to steer wide of any talk of—or reading about—sanctified pain, and I graduated from high school and later from college without ever once having opened Butler. It was probably one of my more costly mistakes.

As a result, I was ill prepared many years later for dealing with what was to happen to Sam and me. At two weeks of age, our second son and fifth child died of pneumonia.

6. Often republished, and occasionally rewritten by Faulkner, "The Bear" first appeared in the *Saturday Evening Post*, May 9, 1942. The version quoted here is from *The Portable Faulkner*, ed. Malcolm Cowley (New York: Viking Press, 1965), 243.

Months after the violent passing, still numb and purposeless, we left the other children with our mothers and went off together on a kind of winter retreat or sabbatical in the mountains, hoping to discover there the energy and the perspective that would let us begin again.

It was the third or fourth day of our time there, and I was feeling more at peace than I had for weeks. The afternoon itself was cozily damp, and the mountains around us were glorious in their fog and drizzle. The secondhand bookstore where we were browsing was charming and quiet. A teakettle, if you can believe it, even simmered on the potbellied stove in the back. The whole village, in fact, was straight out of a brochure, but I was greatly in need of clichés. I was even beginning to trust them. Then suddenly, there on the shelf in front of me, was Butler—a bit mildewed, but there. Invulnerable at last, or so I thought, I picked him up and began to read.

I had always known that whatever else saints may be about, they are most certainly about suffering. What I had never known is that saints are those who neither need their pain nor value it nor ask anything of it. Butler's saints asked of misfortune no cosmic meaning and no personal gain. Indeed, as I stood there reading page after page, it was not the denial of pleasure or the pursuit of poverty or the desire for martyrdom (which things I had always assumed marked a saint), but the letting go that seemed to characterize Butler's heroes. It was, as a discovery, a great shock to my new equilibrium, one I deeply resented at the time.

I had discovered that in real pain, and in genuine grief, there was a kind of immunity from more pain or even from much engagement. Having suffered, I felt that I would not have to suffer again for a long, long time—perhaps even for the rest of my life. I had bought my peace the hard way. Even more, because I had hurt and still was hurting, I knew I was alive. I could touch that pain and be reassured by it, could flatter myself that it had some meaning beyond bacteria and medical accident. I even dredged up Aeschylus and persuaded myself that I had indeed gained wisdom through all of this. After all, these were the insights that our friends and family had sent us to the mountains to achieve.

But there was Butler with his tales of men and women who didn't have to hold on to their pain, who didn't need it to buy themselves immunity from life, who didn't find the reassurance of their own worth in it. Why? Butler seemed to be saying that it was because they every one—to a man and to a woman—believed themselves to have already been validated by God's pain; they believed that all those things I was asking of my grief had already been provided by divine grief. They had let go. I could not. It was the first time I had ever understood the necessity for his "Eloi, Eloi, lama sabachthani!" (Mark 15:34).

I put Butler back on the shelf and left the store. It was only ten minutes later, back in our room, that I realized I had also left Sam, but it didn't matter. He took my absentmindedness as a sure sign of returning health, for absentmindedness has always characterized me as surely as better qualities have characterized the saints.

We left the next day. I couldn't bear all that pseudo-Tyrolean resort décor and said so rather forcefully. Sam laughed. It was the first time, I realized, that I had heard him laugh in weeks.

We came back to our lives and our children. In time we found The Farm in Lucy, bought it, and moved here. The ache for the boy who never grew up on it is no bigger and no smaller than it was all those years ago, just quieter and less arrogant—which is as much instruction and relief as any of us has any right to hope for from stories of other people's faith—at least in faith's beginning.

—*Wisdom in the Waiting,* chapter 12

* * *

Two poems: the first, continuing the theme of meditations upon death, in the tradition of that tremendous line of Cranmer's from the Book of Common Prayer: "In the midst of life we are in death." Then, another short poem, untitled and previously unpublished (I have titled it "A Ditty") on the droll everydayness of domestic life—another central theme in the writing of Tickle's midlife.

The Wake

When we were young,
the children small,
my fingers felt along
the fringes of their face.
My palms went flat at birth
to learn the curvings of their chests.

There are bonds that seal by hand.

So I dress you now,
smooth your hair,
close your lids,
and they must understand:

There are bonds that seal by hand.

A Ditty

Water lines in dark commodes
And dirty rings in bathtub drains,
Spotted Grecoes on my polished pipe . . .
These, my boy, are the parts of you
I'll gladly give a wife.

* * *

This reflection upon the subtle, multivarious religious influences of childhood things was a surprise to many of Tickle's Christian readers, who preferred to consider her without other loyalties, when it first appeared toward the beginning of God-Talk in America, *published during her tenure at* Publishers Weekly. *Three more selections follow, the first also from* God-Talk. *The second is selections from an essay on Mardi Gras, and the last is a complete essay written in the early 1980s, continuing (and completing) the theme.*

MY CHILDHOOD GODS

My earliest experiencing of spiritual intimacy . . . was in the closet that opened off of my first bedroom in the asymmetrical, amorphous way of leftover spaces in old houses.

Huge in its dimensions and cavernous with its ten-foot ceiling, my childhood's closet was sufficiently removed from the household flow as to be only infrequently remembered by anybody but me. It was, in other words, a repository for the curious nonessentials of the adults around me—full of mothballs and almost-dispatched toys, the scent of my mother's perfume still caught in out-of-season clothes, of cedar boxes and of my father's collection of newspapers . . . one for every day of the Second World War from Pearl Harbor to Hiroshima.

Despite its ungainly architecture, everything within the closet was planned and preserved for its utility. Even its shelves were so spaced as to make an uneasy ladder up to the forbidden trapdoor that opened onto insulation and crawl space. And it was always, from the beginning, in the closet that I arranged and stored myself as well. I was the one who threw out its excess, wrought order upon its collections, sorted its debris for the raw materials of my soul's education. Whatever parent or cousin or time dumped, I sorted by feel in the unelectrified dark or by stealth with a flashlight, spiriting out the useless to the alley trash bins and climbing to the top-shelf repository with the remains. There neither my short-of-stature mother nor my taller but less inquisitive father ever could or would go.

The closet was pantheon for my childhood's gods. It was as full of personalities as was my father's copy of the *Inferno*, illustrated by Doré and secreted years before on the upper shelf, much to my father's recurring puzzlement. The upper shelf's walls sang with awesome pictures of Shiva, Astarte, Hecate, Medusa, all torn from the pages of my grandmother's discarded *Chamber's Illustrated Encyclopedia*. A china Ferdinand the Bull (mine were the golden years of Disney) that my uncle had brought me from New York shared the closet's fantasia with crayoned tracings of satyrs much less benign than those Walt Disney would have had me believe in. And the arms of the goddess Kali (brass and beautiful from India, but an adult gift repugnant to my mother who had thrown her away) waxed over the whole of the shelf in constant incantation.

Somewhere just near the attic crawl-through was God the Father. His beard was frequently no more than a cobweb; but still He was there, or passage to Him was. Even as a child I knew that there was no God the Mother and was glad. I did not want one. Gentleness, nurture, support, stroking were sexless in my understanding, belonging to neither gender exclusively and to both identically. It was Kali with her many-handed sexuality whom I wanted as the Queen of Forever. In my imagination she would travel the god's body and mine in sweet sensation while fantasy honed the diffuse appetites of youth into focus.

Kali was, in fact, the only one of the closet's treasures to escape its destruction. She alone still sits on my bedroom dressing table. All the rest have long since gone as victims to my maturing or the house's new owners. I threw Shiva and Astarte away before I was fully ten years old. In high school I had to study Dante and, for convenience, moved him back to the more accessible bookcase. Doré's ghouls and phantasmagoria by that time were more eternally etched into my faith than they ever could have been into the pages of any book. Ferdinand I had broken one adolescent day by slinging him against a brick wall. In a rush of need to know what it was to kill someone I truly loved, I had hurled him away from me. Even today I can still feel the slick heat of him as he slid from my hand to his multifaceted destruction. Like so many toys for so many children, he served better in death than in life, and I never mourned him. Bit by bit and doll by doll, the other treasures were carried out and dispersed to other children, to nieces, nephews, neighbors, some even to my own children.

During Vietnam and not long before his death, my father burned his World War II collection. He had always believed in fairness, made a kind of goddess out of freedom, referring to both of them as "her." When he burned the newspapers, I suspected that he had at last lifted the skirts of idealism and found to his horror a freemartin, a mandrake without parts. After his funeral and before my mother sold the old house, I sorted out and emptied the closet for the last time, keeping back only the Kali but moving it to a much more public place on my dresser. Now only the outline of the never-tested trapdoor and the odor of my mother's perfume remain when I push back to remember the closet.

Each time I go back to remember, of course, the perfume grows more faint, more lost in the loss of odor that is memory. Once the perfume has gone, only the trap door and the going where in time I never went will still be left to me. And after that, Kali will bless a bed on which I no longer am, her brass and my self having changed places with each other for the last time.

* * *

RELIGION IS MY PASSION

I was sixty-two years old the spring I went to Rome for the first time. . . .

. . . Not only was I physically well into late middle age, I was, by profession, an experienced traveler—an experienced experiencer, in fact—trained to look with a calculating eye and think with a suspicious head. All of them are qualities that, having been fiscally reinforced over the years of my working life, tend toward a kind of blaséness and sometimes even to a truly dangerous objectivity that threatens to strip the significance from reality. But beyond those learned and acquired ways of engaging the world I am paid to watch, I was not a naïf in matters of the spirit either.

Religion is my beat only because religion is and always has been my passion. From my earliest memories in my mother's house, religion, mystery, a sure intimacy with an actuality beyond, a third eye or the flick of the vision seen out of the corner of a physical eye—these things have always been there for me. I have served them as a Christian and believed, as I still do, that it is in Christianity only that I can approach and serve them.

That does not mean that I have not recognized intellectually and emotionally the similarities of religious experience among all peoples nor that I have not been schooled in the varying organized religious expressions of millions of other people. Obviously I have, just as I have read literally hundreds—and, I hope, read with empathy and most assuredly with personal benefit—of the spiritual journals, diaries, and manuals of many, many who, like me, have seen and felt and served, though invoking by other names, that which all my life has called to me.

No, it was not a naïf who, surrounded by a noisy group of fellow travelers, stood at the base of the steps leading up into the Pantheon and gawked. As an adolescent taking my first formal classes in the Latin my mother had so surreptitiously siphoned into my soul, I had early learned to appreciate the relief of opening the next lesson in our textbook and discovering a big, full-page or at least half-page illustration. . . . The only picture of the Pantheon (outside of those in some art history texts) that I can remember ever studying intently was the one in that first-year Latin book. I can remember, oddly enough, flipping the first page of our next lesson, seeing the photo illustration, thinking, "Oh, good, there is one!" followed instantly by, "Lord, that's the ugliest building I ever saw!" which was what I, for my part, was gawking at that afternoon in Rome. The damned thing really *was* the ugliest building I had ever seen.

. . . I went up the steps with a close friend and business associate and with some thirty or forty other tourists who, having recovered from their initial surprise, had given up staring in favor of getting out of the heat. In their jostling, chattering, camera-winding company, I pushed through the huge, stolid doors and was alone, abruptly alone on the dark marble floor, alone in the cool, faintly moist air, alone in the unarticulated dome, alone in that light—that strange, inscrutable light—that was the hole in the humming dome. There was no "other" that was not understood and subsumed in that complete light, and I knew in my moment, as I had known in my closet, that God the Father was there above where I looked and that there was no God the Mother.*

As I moved to stand at the border of the light—I was afraid to enter it out of anxiety that I might distort it—I saw beyond its diffusing the arching stones of the dome itself as they rose in celebration of their own perfection. And caught for all time around the rotunda of their circumference I saw again Kali and Shiva and Astarte, though they had different names and wore the different garb of togas and sandals.

It is impossible to convey to another what the intense moments in one's life really are. Always such brief openings are too interior to be plumbed, too much the constructs of all the experiences of the private life to be generally referenced. But even if that were not true, the complete telling of this one would lie too close to sacrilege for me to try here. It must be enough, instead, to say that in those few minutes I experienced something as profoundly ecstatic as I ever have. I was physically as well as psychically within the mystery, and it is.

* * *

* One of the multitude of points that Harvey Cox makes brilliantly and with stellar economy [in *Fire from Heaven: The Rise of Pentecostal Spirituality, and the Re-Shaping of Religion in the Twenty-First Century* (Reading MA: Addison-Wesley, 1995)] is this sense, in what he calls primal religion and I have begun to privately think of as closet religion, of genderless God. Describing a recent trip of his own to Italy and Sicily to visit Christian congregations, Cox ruminates upon a sermon and says: "This is where the most fundamental revolution is going on because what is being altered is nothing short of what might be called 'the gender of God'"(201). He concludes, as have many of us in the populism camp, that " 'God-the-lover' . . . may already be courting the hearts of unlettered men and women . . . albeit unnoticed by theologians" (202).

DUSKY, BROODING DAYS OF EARLY LENT

. . . When I was an undergraduate, I was taught in some psychology class that the most definitive difference between a philosophy and a religion is that the latter requires the eating of the atonement sacrifice, while the former is revulsed by such notions. It was a hard distinction for me to understand as an adolescent.

Mardi Gras, with its carnival and its homage to the pagan, is the church's recognition of how our faith must develop. It is also a recognition of the spiritual necessity for primordial darkness, and of the uses of the other side of light. It is our chance to remember, one time a year and with sanction, the long way of our coming and the strange way of our arriving. In its own way and when combined with faith, it is one of the most instructive holidays of the church's year.

All of us who arrive at spiritual maturity do so by moving through a progression of faiths and comprehensions. In much the same way, all of us who now walk had first to move through a fairly unoriginal progression of motor skills before we arrived at our walking. In effect, what the spiritual process leaves most of us with is a veritable pantheon of early gods and codes, discarded in our maturity, but essential to our growth—gods and understandings that led us to Easter in the first place. . . .

. . . Pancakes and sausages and carnivals. Fat Tuesdays and ash-marked Wednesdays. Earth time caught in calendars of light and dark beyond human control. Winds and weather read by smoke. Many-handed creatures dancing in fluid pose. These things are the stuff of mysteries, the stuff of the dark, enticing, luminous dreams through which we have come and to which we cannot quite return. They are evidence and agent of a knowing we half remember from childhoods and have half inherited from the genes of our forebears. They are the romance of religion, its texture, the surety that holds the soul in the spirit's dance, and nowhere are they richer or more present for me than in the dusky, brooding days of early Lent.

—*Wisdom in the Waiting,* chapter 2

* * *

FINAL SANITY

The forty penitential weekdays and six Sundays that follow Mardi Gras and precede Easter are the days of greatest calm in the church's year. Since by long centuries of custom the date of Easter is annually determined from the first Sunday after the full moon on or after March 21, the intertwining of physical and spiritual seasons is virtually inevitable. The resulting union of deep winter and holy preparation makes reflection, even penitence, a natural activity.

One night years ago, toward the end of winter, there was a storm, a cold front shifting suddenly and dropping onto us with ferocity and winds that bent down the pine trees along the fence line. Sometime after I went to bed, it tore open the pasture gate. We awoke the next morning to bitter cold and a scattered herd: two pregnant heifers in the front yard, six more in the garden eating up what was left of the turnip greens, and seven others, mostly yearlings, playing at some kind of heifer tag in the windy orchard.

The mud from the previous month's snow was three inches thick. Even frozen, it came laughing up to suck off our boots. We slopped and fell and prodded swollen bellies until, ourselves covered with ooze, we fell onto the broken gate and laughed out loud to the gray dawn skies and the startled blackbirds. We drove the last cows through finally, my son John and I, and repaired the gate right enough, coming in out of the cold with feet so wet and frozen that we couldn't feel them, our nightclothes covered in the half-thawed manure. We stank up the kitchen with the good stench of late winter and of the earth when it is resisting one last cold front with the heat of coming fertility.

Later I stood at the spigot and washed the mud from our boots and felt again, as I do every year at this season, a grief for the passing cold. Looking across the pastures to the pond below, I knew it had indeed been the last storm before the spring, and I wanted to run backward toward the early morning, toward the winds and breaking limbs of the previous night.

"Lenzin," our German ancestors used to call this season, and since then we have called it "Lent." It is a time when Christians decorate stone churches with the sea's color and wrap their priests in the mollusk's purple. It was once a time when all things passed through the natural depression of seclusion, short food supplies, and inactivity, a time when body and land both rested. It is still, in the country, a final sanity before the absurd wastefulness of spring.

Each year at this time it is harder for me to desire butterflies and lilies, even to wish for resurrection. Each year I come a little closer to needing the dullness of the sky and the rarity of a single redheaded woodpecker knocking for grubs in the pine bark. Each year also I come a little closer to the single-mindedness of the drake who, muddy underside showing, waddles now across the ice to the cold center water to wash himself for his mate, all in the hope of ducklings later on.

That year, through the thin, sharp air I could hear the younger children in the barn. They were building tunnels again, making forts from the dried bales of hay. From the yapping I knew that even the dogs had joined in the intricacies that the children's imaginations had contrived. Five-year-old Rebecca chased field mice as her brothers built forts. She would catch another soon and drown it in the water trough with unsullied sadism, feeling only the accomplishment that came from having helped to keep her part of the world in balance.

In the summer, the mice would leave, going back to the fields again, and she would take to pulling everything that bloomed instead, bringing them all in to me indiscriminately. The tin-roofed barn would be stifling, and the hay forts would have all been eaten. The boys would be picking beans and complaining of the itch from the okra leaves, being themselves too hot and tired to desire anything except nightfall and bed. The drake would have a family, which he would abandon to the mate he had so much desired, and the woodpecker's carmine head would burn out to tired tan.

The farm in the summer becomes like the city is all year: too much color, too much noise, too much growing, too much hurry to stave off loss and destruction, too little natural death and gentle ending, too little time for play, too little pointless imagination.

I can remember many summers now; it is the singular advantage of years that one can do so. And I remember that once summer comes, I spend it wallowing in the easiness of it—the excess of its fruits and vegetables, the companionship of summer's constant sounds as the hum of the insects and of the rototillers give way in the evening to the croaking of the frogs and the raucousness of the katydids. I remember also how I would begin early, in that green time of Ordinary Time, to dread the stillness of the coming cold, to fear the weariness of winter menus, the bitterness of breaking open pond water for thirsty cattle, and the packing of lunches—interminable lunches—for reluctant children on their way to school.

But now, years later, it is Lent once again, and for one more snow I can luxuriate in the isolation of the cold, attend laconically to who I am, what I value, and why I'm here. Religion has always kept earth time. Liturgy only gives sanction to what the heart already knows.

—*Wisdom in the Waiting*, chapter 5

* * *

Years later Tickle wrote of the universal appeal of religious symbols, ritual, and language: "Religion is the rope of meaning. . . . The need to not live without rules and connection to something larger is apparently innate and intractable in us. Religion is the salve to that need; and the assuaging of that need is religion." Prayer Is a Place, *87.*

* * *

Two poems from the late 1970s, written on The Farm in Lucy.

Afternoon Social
Lucy Methodist Church

In the orchard
where a herd of shadows
is pasturing
under the apple trees
women
as thin as empty houses
are having tea.

Lucy at Dusk

Our pasture tonight
is the warm teacups
my mother lifted from the water
and set to drain,
their soapy bubbles blinking
on her hands
like fireflies
across our meadow.

—*Selections*

* * *

This commencement address was delivered three months after 9/11. It was first written, then read aloud to an audience. That is an uncommon posture for Tickle. She rarely ever read from more than rough notes when lecturing, and for at least two decades she was lecturing a hundred times a year, often for more than an hour at a stretch. Anyone who has listened to Tickle, or heard her preach, knows there are times when words seem to form in her mouth differently from other times; these are usually occasions of great import, as when she is quoting from Holy Scripture. In The Shaping of a Life *she wrote about her first experience reading aloud from the Psalter as a young woman: "I love to read aloud. I always have. . . . Yet I felt almost immediately that what I was doing was work, work in some part of* *me that had been previously unemployed. . . . there is some muscle involved in sounding words. . . . there is some mental labor expended in trying to connect meaning to words" (*The Shaping of a Life, *48–49).*

COMMENCEMENT ADDRESS, SAMFORD UNIVERSITY DECEMBER 15, 2001

President Corts, Distinguished Deans and Faculty, Ladies and Gentlemen of the Graduating Class, Honored Friends, Family, and Guests:

It would be a privilege to be invited to this campus to speak on any commencement day, but for me it is especially so this December and especially so before this class raduates. Now in our time of human distress and global upheaval, the careers you have prepared yourselves to enter—careers that will, in essence, begin so soon as I sit down and your dean hands each of you the credentialing passport of a Samford or Beeson diploma—those careers have a weightiness and a portent that would have been incomprehensible only three months and one week ago.

As President Corts has already told you, I am a professional religionist. That is to say, I make my living writing and speaking within the field of religion; and certainly there could be no more appropriate year or more appropriate occasion for talking religion than the present one. Not only is this the day of your beginning new and empowered careers in an abruptly disoriented world, but it is also, by some twist of the lunar or the lunar/solar calendar, the confluence this year of the winter holy days for the whole family of the Abrahamic faiths or, in other words, for almost all of us in this room or even in this country, because by professed faith most of us Americans are the religious and spiritual heirs of Father Abraham.

Tomorrow at sunset, if you are Jewish, you will light the eighth and last candle of a menorah somewhere in your home, you will sing the ancient songs of a triumphant Judah and of its holy temple, you will exchange more gifts with those whom you love, you may even eat another latke or two and spin a dreidel one last time, all of which eating and gifting, singing and lighting will mark the closing day of Hanukkah for the year 5762 in your calendar.

Tonight at midnight, if you are Christian, you will commence the third Sunday of the Advent season. Of the four Sundays in that holy time of our waiting, the third is the one that historically has been dearest to the heart of most of the world's Christians, the one most fervently observed and most honored over the centuries. It is the Sunday of the pink candle in the Advent wreath. It is the Sabbath of the Blessed Virgin Mother.

Tomorrow as the sun sets, if you are Muslim, you will watch the sky carefully to sight the new moon, for with the sighting of the new moon, the purifying fast of Ramadan for the year 1380 will come to its end and the joyous breaking of that month-long discipline of self-denial—the rich festal celebration of Eid al-fitr—will begin.

If, then, you this morning are a Jew, a Christian, or a Muslim—and statistically speaking you almost assuredly are one of them by culture and loyalty, if not by personal profession—you are graduating on the eve of a very holy day not only in your branch of the Abrahamic faiths, but indeed in all three of them. In such an unusual joining of events as the next sunrise and sunset hold for all of us, there undoubtedly is much basis for commentary upon the commonality of our shared, monotheistic beginning, and even more room, perhaps, for conversation about the variations upon that theme which distinguish us one from another, variations which even may be said, at times like these, sharply to divide us. Yes, there is much this morning to justify and sustain my offering you a monolog about formal religion.

But what President Corts also told you in his introduction a moment ago, at least implicitly, is that I am by natural inclination as well as trade first and foremost a writer and a teller of tales. So what I want to do this morning is set religion aside just now and simply tell you a story, suspecting as I do so that a story would be much more appealing than a speech to you as well as to me.

Now, for you to understand the story I want to tell, I must first give you some of its circumstances. For example, you need to know that my husband, Sam, and I are both from Tennessee. We both have lived almost all of our lives in that state, even growing up together there, in east Tennessee, over sixty years ago. My own parents were born and reared in the deltalike farmlands of west Tennessee and so were adult transplants to the high hill country of Appalachia; but my husband's mother was seventh generation east Tennessean, her Grandfather Witcher's land at the time of his death still being registered at the county courthouse under an original bill of grant signed by King George III of England.

Mamaw—for so I and all her children and grandchildren called her—Mamaw was a Witcher in a place where that name meant something, in other words. But she was also a disciplined woman, teaching her descendants—my own children especially, for they came last in the progression of her grandchildren—teaching my children to lay responsible claim to the blood they carried and to the heritage they enjoyed. That is undoubtedly part—a large part, in fact—of the reason for their absorption even today with everything Witcher, including the roadside marker on the south side of the Limestone Cove Highway just a bit east by southeast of the little town of Unicoi, Tennessee.

Put there by the state's historical commission, the thick metal sign marks the turn-in to a nineteenth-century cemetery. Still used from time to time for burials and still maintained in a more or less informal way by the community around it, the graveyard is like almost every other country graveyard you have ever seen—treed, cool, and silent. It is, in other words, unremarkable in every way save for the sign just outside its entrance and the commanding mound of a communal grave at its front, northernmost corner.

The historical commission's marker, with its black letters raised up off its silvered surface, says, succinctly: "Here are buried the eight civilians killed at the home of Dr. David Bell in November, 1863. Enroute to Kentucky to join Federal forces, they were found by a detachment of Col. W. A. Witcher's Confederate cavalry, while waiting for breakfast. They were: B. Blackburn, Calvin Cantrel, Elijah Gentry, Jacob Lyons, Wiley Royal, John Sparks and two unknown. Buried nearby is Dr. Bell's brother, James, killed at the same time."

The events of that November morning almost a century and a half ago are referred to locally as either the Limestone Cove Tragedy or as Witcher's Massacre. What the roadside marker does not tell you about, however—what it simply assumes every visitor will know—is that the slayers and the slain of Limestone Cove were all southerners, probably some of them even kin, who were caught in a conflict of such clashing values and opposing moral direction as could only be resolved by war.

In point of actual fact, the W. A. Witcher who was a colonel of the Confederate Cavalry was not Mamaw's forebear, though common sense and mountain isolation make it almost inconceivable that he was not related at some degree of proximity or remove. But kin by an establishable relationship or not, for all the years of their childhood, when we would be in east Tennessee visiting Mamaw and decide to take her out for a family ride, she as often as not would say to Sam, "Let's stop by the cemetery and show the children the marker."

This was not a macabre gesture on her part. In point of fact, it was quite the opposite, for once we were there, she would read our children first the marker itself and then the gravestone on the common grave mound: "They were: B. Blackburn, Calvin Cantrel, Elijah Gentry, Jacob Lyons, Wiley Royal, John Sparks and two unknown." Almost, I can say the litany of their names without having to read them after so many years of hearing them.

But after the reading, our children, and we with them, would turn aside. They went running off as children almost always do when they are set loose in the open spaces of a cemetery; and Sam and I simply wandered away in order to distance ourselves from Mamaw. We wandered, in other words, so as to not intrude on what was to follow.

Always, Mamaw would bend down and pick up some object—a leaf, a twig, a bit of grass, a fallen acorn shell the squirrels had left. She would toy for a minute or two with whatever she had chosen, fingering it as one does with the beads of a prayer chain. Then her fingers would grow quiet, the chosen object sometimes even dropping from them, and her eyes would fill—so full sometimes that the tears welled over and down into the slack of her cheeks, but there were never any words after that. When she was done, she would call to us, saying that we needed to get home for supper and then begin fussing over the children, brushing leaves off one or spit-scrubbing dirt off the hands of another with her handkerchief. It was all over once again.

Now there are a number of things that one can conclude from Witcher's Massacre and the roadside sign that marks the burial site of its victims. The first and most obvious is that ideas are always more powerful than the commonality of either blood or place. They always have been and presumably always will be. The second is that had the South won the War Between the States, the roadside marker would announce "The Site of Witcher's Victory" and history would talk about "The Rout at Limestone Cove." Cynical as such a statement may sound, we deny the irony of it to our own peril. None of us can afford ever to forget that the tale pivots in accord with who the victor is.

The third in my list of possible conclusions is gentler, nearer to compassion than to survival. It is the understanding that in war there is never a right or a wrong which does not have its other and opposite side. Only with the passage of time do the issues involved in any war come to seem unadulterated, inherent, and clear.

As an old woman—one almost as old now as my late mother-in-law was then—I can also say, and hope you will accept as palatable, that death always buys something. Both the heroes and the antagonists of Limestone Cove, by their actions and their dying, tore away the mores and patterns of one way of life and thereby brought about a more moral, more equitable, more just way of being for more people, themselves as well as their opponents. This was true in their case not necessarily because they as individuals wanted to pursue a course of massacre and violation as such—almost certainly, that is, not because they wanted as individuals to be killed and, most probably for most of the men under Colonel Witcher's command, not because they truly wished to kill—but because every one of them on that November morning was part of an epoch and an outmoded human social construct that had run their courses.

And, as a kind of footnote, the journalist in me must add to my list as well the observation that bits of the quotidian like "killed . . . waiting for breakfast" are always worthy of our fierce respect. Juxtaposed to copy one way, they are morally suspect because they prejudice by their selective use of a minor fact; positioned in another, they become the keys to the kingdom which is good copy.

Now having said all of that, I must push on to say that not for one minute do I think—nor did I ever think—that Mamaw was preoccupied with any of these thoughts as she stood in front of the burial mound at Limestone Cove and wept so soundlessly. What she was doing instead—and what we understood at the time that she was doing—was stopping a while before a void into which no words can go. Created by violence, the cemetery at Limestone Cove was and remains a deceptively bucolic passageway into an eternal interruption that is beyond interruption, that is itself complete. It was this and this alone before which I always thought my mother-in-law stood and wept; or I did until the day she said to me, "It is so good to be here."

The cemetery at Limestone Cove is the smallest and humblest of all small and humble historical sites, so much so in fact that I would be amazed if any of you save my husband in front here had ever heard of if before this morning. And as for Witcher's Massacre, it was, I will wager, the very smallest and least revered of all the bloody engagements that made the War Between the States the bloodiest and most deadly war in American history.

Today we have—all of us in this country—another cemetery. We were given it like a wound to our bodies in mid-September. The two sites could not be more dissimilar: the nineteenth century one is small, rural, infrequently seen, completely resolved; the twenty-first century one, huge beyond our imagining, exquisitely urban, quietly but constantly visited even after sunset, and is years, perhaps decades, from resolution. Eventually, of course, when we come to post the list of those who were interrupted there, our list, like that of Limestone Cove's, will contain the names of men and women who were made into heroes one fall morning simply because they stopped too long or not long enough in waiting for their breakfast. But violence and some caprice of diurnal timing are not the only threads of similarity binding our two, disparate graveyards together. There is at least one other.

One day in mid-October—on Thursday, October 16th, to be exact—Sam and I made our first pilgrimage to Ground Zero. We got out of a cab at Rector Place and walked a block northeast to Trinity Wall Street. The barricades that cordon off the acres of destruction created by 9/11 wrap around the southeastern corner of Trinity's churchyard, and we began walking them there, walking slowly northward, walking with dozens and dozens of other sorrow-filled people. Ash and debris were everywhere, the odor of smoke from the burning buildings pervasive; but so too was the silence. There was no sound . . . no traffic, no commerce, certainly, but more tellingly, there was no conversation amongst us who walked save for an occasional "Excuse me" or "Can you see around me?" Men and women alike were crying, but crying as soundlessly and unguardedly as once I had watched Mamaw cry.

As Sam and I got a bit more than halfway up the mile or so of barricades, the odor of smoke grew sharper, and we could hear the occasional disturbance of a jack hammer working in the rubble. We could also feel the rain, except that it was not raining.

The day was cloudless; nonetheless, there was a light mist falling both inside and just along the outer edges of the barriers. Like everyone else moving along the cordons, I stopped and looked up in confusion only to determine first that indeed there was no rain and then to discover the source of the falling mist.

Three or four teams of workmen were cleaning the buildings of Ground Zero. Twenty, thirty, perhaps even forty stories above our heads, a dozen or so men were hosing the windows and exterior facings of buildings that, while still structurally useable, were none the less too cloaked in ash and soot to be habitable.

Almost immediately, however, my attention was drawn away from watching the workmen above me and back to the people surrounding me. One after another, as each perceived what was happening, he or she began to edge quietly forward and lean into the ashy mist, receiving it like a baptism upon outstretched hands and upturned faces. And as they did so, I heard Mamaw's voice saying across the years, "It is so good to be here."

Ground Zero and Limestone Cove are places of aggregate and orchestrated death, of civilian death in the face of war, and because of those two fundamental similarities between them, the goodness of being in one is the goodness of being in the other. Neither our minds, with their imaginations and endless chattering, nor our bodies with their mortal fears and necessities can survive for long in a place of so many and such deliberate interruptions. Yet our loss and the violation to our sense of fair expectations draw us to try—dare us even to stare at this rip in the curtain of our understanding, this enervating rupture in the stabilizing shell of our minds' perceptions and our bodies' dimensions.

Like October mourners leaning their hands and faces for cleansing into water made holy by pollution, we lean closer and closer toward the rifts of both Limestone Cove and the World Trade Center until our awareness, slips, bereft of our wills, into them and we stand gazing into the dark—the luminous, all-receiving dark. We stand, as once upon another time my mother-in-law used to do, at the margin between the worlds and, like her, gaze in upon the evidence of things not presently seen and the substance of things now hoped for.

Which brings me full circle, of course, and us back to religion, because my story ends in that luminous, all-receiving dark—in the beauty beyond articulation which is the wellspring of all religion. It ends in faith. And on any day or in any year, I would hold faith out to each of you who are graduating today as both map and tool in the work that lies ahead of you; but I do so even more passionately this December morning. In time, it may be said of some of you that you came too soon to your breakfast; of others, that you came too late; and of others of you, perhaps nothing at all. But for all of you, it is the work of Ground Zero and the writing of its story that lie ahead and that, for your generation, are an unavoidable labor. For the sake of all of these things, then, I beg you, take faith with you from this place and, may it please God, use it both carefully and well as you do so; for if you do, when all the cordons are gone and all the barriers are at last removed, your children's children, like mine, will be able to stand staring into Ground Zero and to say, "It is so good for us to be here."

* * *

The following two pieces represent Tickle's passion for the Christian story and Christian formation.

SIX ESSENTIALS FOR PASSING ON THE FAITH

Train up a child in the way s/he shall go etc., etc. may be the oldest cliché that parents are subjected to in this world. It certainly is the most annoying when it is laid upon one by an overweening grandparent. Yet there is—isn't there always!—a rock-solid truth in the whole thing. In this case, what it means is that the first thing we must do in teaching and forming our children is to become dreadfully honest with ourselves and our mates and/or extended family about just how Christian we want this youngster to be and in what ways.

Most of us, if we're honest, eventually conclude this preliminary work by realizing that what we really want to form is not so much a code of conduct, though that is obviously important, as it is an intimacy with God and the things of God. What we want to implant is an easy and natural affection for the holy, an inherent connectedness to an ongoing story and a sense of membership within a sustaining community that, being larger than any of us, is always there to hold all of us as well as demand some things of us.

And to do these things, the second step is to pray earnestly together as parents and/or extended family, and without the children present, for them and for the progress of their souls. That, too, seems like a no-brainer, but it is an adult or mentoring habit often overlooked and almost never routinized in the press of other, more immediate duties.

The third on my short list of a half-dozen essentials is a bit easier to accomplish. Children respond (as do we all) to the very business of routine, and here the flow of the week itself helps. Judaism long ago discovered the informing necessity not just of observing Sabbath—really observing it, that is—but also of wrapping it in prayerful preparation and prayerful conclusion. What that translates to for us is a time of evening prayer as a family on the eve of Sabbath and again on the evening of the Sabbath itself, the former to be a time of preparation for communal worship, and the latter to be a time of family thanksgiving for having been granted the gift thereof.

The fourth in my short list of essentials is storytelling, but there is a trick here, too. It is a good and joyful thing to read to children (or watch a DVD rendition thereof with them), but it is not nearly as instructive as is the business of telling them a story without benefit of books or discs. Implied in telling is the authenticity of what is being told. The underlying message is that this story matters. It matters because Daddy or Granddaddy or Uncle Bill knows it all the way through. It matters because Mama or Granny or Aunt Sue loves it enough to know exactly what happens next. Of course, what that also means—and this is the source of the child's perception of authenticity—is that Daddy and Mama et al. have valued this story enough to know it in detail and have also thought about it before telling it. What telling rather than reading or watching also means, of course, is that the stories of the faith can be pulled out spontaneously when their words and plot lines are apropos of some conversation or situation other than bedtime.

All of that is to say that I suspect that of all the things we do in shaping our children in the faith, it is the storytelling that is most formative over the long years of their adult lives. I also think (which is far beyond "I suspect," obviously) that one of the things we as mentoring Christians need most urgently to turn our energies toward is adult classes in teaching each other how to be good storytellers and then in learning in detail the stories of both the Hebrew and the Christian scriptures that most need our telling.

The fifth thing in my short list of ways and means is music. In religion, it is, always and finally, the music that instructs the spirit and rides with it through the years. If we need adult classes in the stories of the faith and the art of their telling, then just as surely we need training sessions with one another about the beloved songs that are our heritage, about intentional ways to bring them seamlessly into domestic life, about family songfests, certainly, but even more about tunes woven artlessly into the mundane business of our lives together.

And last in my half dozen is something even more basic than storytelling and singing. That is, if there is anything that appeals to a child more than those, it is food. In fact, food manages to leave a fairly lasting impression on all of us, and this is especially true of food that is tied, on an ongoing basis, to special events. We hear "Easter" and think "eggs," whether we want to or not. Of course, the other side of that associative process is that, because we all love Christmas candy, when we see a peppermint stick, we inevitably think "Christmas" whether it's Christmas or not. Our forebears in the faith used to use that double reinforcement of food and event more or less un-self-consciously; but it is an art, a grace, and a legitimate ploy that we have somehow lost or misplaced along the way.

The story of the Church herself, the grand narrative of the beloved community and the body of Christ on earth, is tied to more events than Christmas and Easter. It is tied to Shrove Tuesday with its pancakes for supper and the tale behind the pancakes. It is tied to a lovely cake in early January from the midst of which colored ribbons rise and trail along the sides, just waiting for the lucky child who will be the one to pull out the wondrous streamer with the tiny, tiny baby doll attached—just waiting for the happy remembrance of this day when Mary and Joseph took their baby son to the Temple and gave him there, before the priest, his Holy Name of Jesus. It is cinnamon buns on Good Friday, bearing their cross as they come to us bitter-sweet in their remembrance, etc.

These, then, are for me the sacred half dozen from which all other efforts and intentions and programs must depend. Small and domestic though they may be, it is nonetheless by means of them that we begin to instill into the young the faith of our fathers and mothers. And of course, it is by the employment of them for our children that we teach and renew ourselves, even as we are teaching them.

—originally written as part of a Patheos symposium,
"Passing on the Faith: Teaching the Next Generation,"
first published on August 1, 2013, at patheos.com

* * *

BIBLE STORIES YOUR MOTHER NEVER TOLD YOU

Folks in my line of work . . . do a lot of talking and lecturing during the fall, winter, and spring months when schools are in session and everyone more or less agrees that vacation time is over and done with for another year. Why exactly it is that the school year still determines vacation and play time for the whole of society has never been terribly clear to me, but I do recognize the immutability of the system.

During the summer months, however, when no one wants a lecture series or special weekends of emphasis or whatever, the job description for my tribe changes from writer and speaker to homilist—or it does if one knows how to make that transition. I, unfortunately, will never make a preacher, much less a homilist. I'll talk to any body of still bodies, and with real pleasure in the doing of it, but preach I can't. Instead, I tell stories, which is a roundabout way of saying that I manage still to do something much nearer to a lecture than a homily ever will be.

Last Sunday, pray God, was my last this summer for playing the role of pseudo- or faux-homilist. Most of the clergy folk I know are now settling back into place and gearing up for the year ahead. Now normally, I would be sighing a sigh of relief, wiping my brow dramatically, and settling in to the usual late-July/early August pattern of preparing for September and the lecture trail. For some reason, though, I have not been able to do that this past week, and I think my hang-up has to do with last Sunday's story.

For years, I have said to publishers that someone needs to put out a volume of Bible Stories Your Mother Never Told You, a collection of stories about the grit and the realism and grandeur of the Bible as it is, not as we have sanitized and trimmed it to be. But there is also another book I have only recently begun to say needs badly to be written. That one is a collection of all the Bible Stories Your Mother Should Have Told You To Read.

The most dangerous thing that can happen to a religion, much less to those who follow it, is for that religion to become socially acceptable. Once that initially welcomed shift in cultural acceptance has occurred, so too has the process of secularization, accommodation, and enculturation begun. Probably the most tragic and complete example of that progression in all of human history is the evolution of Christianity in the West after Constantine. And always, the thing above all others that must be debilitated or deactivated in such a process is the stories that have carried the faith and melded the community of believers into a body of the faithful.

Story is a function of time—or Time, if that is a clearer naming of the thing. Story requires memory, and memory requires time. Story, not thinking, is the thing that separates us from the other creatures with whom we share the universe. It is not only that we have to retain and readily access the past, but also that we have to be able to access or conceptualize a future, if we are to live in time. And the minute we do those things, we have story. Not fact, but story. Persuade us, though, that facts are real in terms of Now and stories are ephemera of Elsewhere and Whenever, and we fall rudderless into a sea of roiling and disconnected events.

In order to enculturate or assimilate a religion completely, therefore, a social unit must be very sure to accomplish two things: it must suppress the bulk of the religion's not-so-nice stories; and it must somehow manage to domesticate the embedded stories that are too gripping or—even worse—are in violation of the society's worldview, common good, and general stability. Bible stories like that of Tamar or Jephthah's daughter fall in the first category, but Daniel in the lions' den or Noah and his ark fall into the second.

It was the story of Noah and his ark that I told last Sunday and that has played in my head all this whole week since. Noah, who was the first vintner—a very noble acquisition of skills, may I add, and much appreciated, at least at our house. Noah, who was the first to whom God gave animal flesh to eat, rather than simple grains and vegetables—not so universally lauded at our place.

Noah, to whom the Noachide Covenant or the Seven Laws of Noah were given and upon which, on March 20, 1991, the Congress of the United States was pleased to proclaim, as signed by President Bush, that this country was founded.

Noah, who rode the waves of shift from prehistory into the general configuration of the earth as we know it. Noah, whose actions opened up the way for the creation of the doctrine of the Righteous Gentile.

Noah, whose name itself means "comfort" or "relief" and at whose birth it was said that he would grant surcease to people in our kind's toils upon a cursed earth. Noah, whose faith through the forty days of rain and the forty days of waiting in the water for a dove to return, prefigured Moses's passage through the waters of the Red Sea and Israel's forty years in the wilderness, and the baptism of Messiah followed immediately by his own forty days of torment in the desert. That Noah, whose passage is reenacted at the baptism of every Christian.

That Noah, who is not a fact or a non-fact or even anywhere in the neighborhood of that construct of human function. Noah who dwells in story and is therefore. Noah who should never have been reduced to a child's toy or a silly rhyme about a floody-floody for children of the Lord. Noah whose grandeur and drama haunt me this Sabbath morning, for he stretches from then to here and from there to me. I am glad this Lord's Day for his abiding presence; and I am glad beyond all saying for the Story.

—originally published on Jim Wallis's "God's Politics" blog, *Sojourners*, July 23, 2008

* * *

Last, we see Tickle making it clear that, despite our species' complicated ways of deconstructing what it means to be human, leaving "old" religious understandings behind for "new" sophistications, some things remain true.

SOMETHING IT IS IN US THAT SINS

Whether one be a Christian or an adherent of another of the Abrahamic faiths or even whether one be a theist or nontheist or atheist, however, one still must acknowledge the presence of that which appears to be—has indeed always been held to be—universally human. We must confess, each of us, that the human animal seems to come into the experience of time constructed and equipped not only with body parts and consciousness, but also with inescapable companions of the interior that historically we have often referred to as our demons. While that term may be etymologically accurate, it is no longer popularly so; for "demon," from the time when Jewish and Christian writers first usurped it until very recently, has incontestably connoted evil or destructiveness in popular usage, whereas the truth is that these taunting companions of ours can prod us into well-being as well as destruction. Indeed without them we will die just as because of them we are condemned to die. They are usually listed as being seven in number, these invisible companions of ours, and the conundrum they posit is the second death from which the Christian seeks salvation just as surely as they are the torment from which the Buddhist seeks release in his or her search for nothingness through the subjugation of desire.

Despite all the eons of human struggle, however, and under the rubrics of any faith, the seven still reenter our being with the birth of every child; and with every new child, we, as coinhabitants of time, and they, as emerging agencies of time, must engage all over again the intricacy of the seven and their chameleonlike ability to change from virtue to vice and back again in the wink of an eye. Without the fascinating seven, we human beings would never rest or eat or procreate or build or aspire. We would also, however, never sedate ourselves with drugs or gorge or suffer an epidemic of AIDS; nor, for that matter, would we murder, steal, or lie. Without them, we would not, in other words, be human; for we are instruments of a tension held in place by, and ticking in place only because of, the arc or slide of the pendulum between the virtues of courage, faith, fortitude, love, hope, prudence, and justice and their corresponding alter egos of pride, envy, anger, lust, sloth, gluttony, and greed.

Christianity, the predominant religious system in the West, calls those seven vices the seven deadly sins and has since its beginnings in Galilee. The interchangeability of vice with sin may not be exclusively a Christian foible, but it is most certainly an inelegant one for the rest of the world's faith communions in that it blurs the line between what is universal in humanity's construction and the exercise of an act that does not, in and of itself, have to be. But whether a religious system conflates or separates vice and sin, the truth remains that every system from Hinduism to Christianity has agreed over the centuries that of our seven demons, greed is the mistress.

—*Greed,* 11–12

3

Prayer—Fixed-Hour and Otherwise

Lent

St. Anne's Parish, Lucy, Tennessee

We must think now
in this time of winter.
We must stop
and we must consider—
what is this sleep
we fear to enter?
We must think now
and we must consider
what it is
that we must consider
while the wind sweeps
the gutters and the streets
now in this time of winter.
When the mind sleeps,
the body wearies and grows bitter.
We must stop now
and consider,
before the lilies rise,
why the god denies
an easy sleep.
We must stop now
and we must consider
what it is that can be lost to us

if the will should balance and wither
now
in this time of winter.

—*Selections*

* * *

This chapter contains what most Phyllis Tickle readers knew of her authorship in the late 1990s and the early years of the twenty-first century: she was the person who brought fixed-hour prayer to a wide, popular, not-necessarily-churched audience. In her time at Publishers Weekly *she often spoke of books becoming "portable pastors"; then, when she left* Publishers Weekly, *she demonstrated how this can happen, turning fixed-hour prayer into a common spiritual practice. But long before the first of* The Divine Hours, *Tickle was a woman of prayer and a writer preoccupied with the subject.*

*The following reflection comes from one of her works of religion journalism, and occurs in that work just after she's written about a colleague who informs her that Christian pastors are teaching their flocks to wrap themselves in traditional prayer shawls, or tallith, "that is, that Jesus was a Jew and the tallit was His closet." Among other things, this demonstrates Tickle's affection for Judaism, a religious tradition that has fed her second only to Christianity. She has written in various places about this, as when she reflects on working among Jews in Memphis as a young woman and how it taught her to understand Jesus: "As 'the Word among us' Jesus made no sense to me and had no appeal. As Torah among us, he was breathtaking." (*The Shaping of a Life, *259)*

PRAYING IN CLOSETS

"And whenever you pray, do not be like the hypocrites; for they love to stand and pray in the synagogues and at the street corners, so that they may be seen by others. Truly I tell you, they have received their reward.

> But whenever you pray, go into your room and shut the door and pray to your Father who is in secret; and your Father who sees in secret will reward you.
>
> "When you are praying, do not heap up empty phrases as the Gentiles do; for they think that they will be heard because of their many words. Do not be like them, for your Father knows what you need before you ask him.
>
> "Pray then in this way: Our Father in heaven, hallowed be your name. . ." (from Matthew 6).

The most beloved and most-used liturgical text in Christian practice pivots around a closet . . . and if in a time of standardized construction the place of that prayer must change from the privacy of irregular walls to the tenting of prayer shawls, it matters not at all. What matters is that the communion and petitions of each worshiper's faith first be solitary and that in their privacy of place these exercises of the individual heart stay ever mindful of their connectedness to the general principles of monotheistic faith: divine, familial love: *Our Father*; the assertion of belief: *Who art in heaven*; the use of reverence and awe: *Hallowed be Thy name*; the declaration of greater qualities: *Thy Kingdom come*; a readiness to submission: *Thy will be done on earth as it is in heaven*; the hope of expectant request: *Give us this day our daily bread*; the two-edged practice of a reciprocal and truly frightening repentance: *And forgive us our trespasses as we forgive those who have trespassed against us*; and the security of ecstatic praise: *For Thine is the kingdom and power and the glory forever and ever. Amen.* Whatever happens after that *Amen* happens as a result of the whole.

—from the final "Interlude" in *God-Talk in America*

* * *

WHEN ANSWERS WITHER THE ELEGANCE OF A MYSTERY

I have a son-in-law—actually Sam and I have four sons-in-law—a great treasury of good men bringing strength and affection to our lives, but I have one son-in-law whose own mother died not too many months ago. As one would expect, he and our daughter made two or three trips back to his home after that death, and they did with sorrow and peace all the things that human passing requires of those of us who love and have been loved.

One of those trips back home—the last one in fact—was to close down the old home place, emptying it of the personal effects that had been his mother's life and his own childhood, dividing goods and memorabilia amongst all the siblings, cleaning the remaining shell of home for resale to some other family. Several weeks after that most painful week of rending and leave-taking, our daughter came into my office one day and laid on my desk a piece of paper. "We wanted you to have this," she said, "because we thought you would care for it the way Dorothy did. She kept it with her all the time."

What my daughter had sat on my desk was actually a photocopy, but even in photocopy, it was clear that the original of which this was the image had been well-worn and, indeed, carried into Dorothy's daily life. Here, then, is what she had so valued, the prayer-poem she had so honored.

Lovely Lady

Lovely Lady dressed in blue,
Teach me how to pray!
God was just your little Boy.
Tell me what to say!
Did you lift Him up sometimes,
Gently on your knee?
Did you sing to Him the way

Mother does to me?
Did you hold his hand at night?
Did you ever try
Telling Him stories of the world?
Oh! And did he ever cry?
Do you really think He cares
If I tell Him things—
Little things that happen?
And do the Angels' wings
Make a noise? And can He hear
Me if I speak low?
Does He understand me now?
Tell me—for you know.
Lovely Lady dressed in blue,
Teach me how to pray!
God was just your little Boy,
And you must know the way!

They were right, of course, our daughter and son-in-law. I do treasure their gift. I carry it now, in fact, or more correctly, I carry a photocopy of their photocopy sealed in clear plastic in my breviary. I treasure Dorothy's prayer. I have to call it Dorothy's for there is no indication on my copy of where she found it or of who originally wrote it. I treasure Dorothy's prayer-poem as a mother, for of all the gifts my adult sons and daughters have given me in the years of their maturity, I can think of few that have sunk with greater meaning into my own life, nor can I think of any that have more touched me with their candor and grace.

But just as my daughter also knew and understood in making their gift, I treasure the Lovely Lady as a professional religionist as well as a mother and mother-in-law. That is to say, that for one who like me makes her living as an observer of and commentator upon religion, the Lovely Lady is a proof text of sorts of where many Americans, observant Christians or cultural Christians or just would-be Christians, where many Americans are yearning to be. What the Lovely Lady prayer speaks to—the reason she so moves my heart and so presumably moved and sustained Dorothy's—is that, as a picture poem, it carries our Lord to complete humanness.

Dorothy's poem assumes the most fundamental of human relationships, that of mother with child, and then assumes from there all of the normal emotions for God that inform human childhood. What the prayer does, in other words, is almost naively, but very persuasively, give us a God who has an emotional life. Such a daring feat becomes a shocking one when it is pulled out and articulated for what it is, but buried in the innocence of a small poem, such a feat becomes a shrewd and small, but mighty, miracle.

What Dorothy's poem subtly does is jump all the barriers of the centuries. In two dozen lines of very ordinary verse, it removes the encumbrances of two thousand years of doctrine and distance. Doctrine and distance, blessedly, have given us who are here today the incarnate God who is Christ, but they have also sealed away from our hearts and from all immediacy the vulnerable human being who was the Incarnation itself. Even those of us who know and walk with Jesus, and say so in just those terms every day, cannot know the inside corridors and mansions of His own interior life. They are blocked to us, they are nowhere recorded for us, they are forever a barrier between us. Only He knew them—He and the Lovely Lady.

The centuries have given Christians the divinity of Christ. Mary, as always, gives contemporary Christians a bridge of connection with His ancient and original humanity. It is a connection, an intimacy in knowing, a consoling comfort in identity, that fills the hearts of thousands today who yearn to find the heat and flesh of the God they hold in their thoughts to be the Son of God. In this, my daughter was correct. But it is as an observant Christian, more than as a mother or as a professional observer, that I treasure her gift of the rhymed prayer.

There is much discussion amongst us these days about the Virgin Birth. In fact, I suspect that few, if indeed any, of the historic tenets of our faith are under anything like the barrage of skepticism and revisionism that is presently assaulting the twelve verses from the Gospel of Luke that are our appointed scripture for this Christmas Sunday. That concerns me deeply as a Christian. It concerns me because, for Christians, belief or disbelief in the Virgin Birth has become a point of division and of mutual scorn that eats away at the far more fundamental imperative of Christian love. It concerns me as well because so long as we Christians are ourselves pinioned and flailing on the spikes and stakes of our scornful divisiveness, we become a human fence between our non-Christian friends and neighbors and the faith which we say we wish to offer them.

The truth in both our camps is that no one knows. As with the infant needs and adolescent emotions and young adult interior of Jesus of Nazareth, only He and the Lovely Lady know what really happened. Only they, too, know by what means and machinations He really came to be among us. Once, in adulthood, He Himself addressed this, I think, if I read correctly, with a good deal of relish and perhaps some humor.

On that occasion, He had just been tested three times in a row in a public forum by the religious leaders of his day and by their cleverly contrived questions of dogma and practice. After He had rendered his answers to their questions—presumably with success—He turned, while they were still all together, and took them on with a dogma/doctrine question of His own.

"What do you think of Messiah?" he asked them. "Whose Son is He?"

"Why, David's," they answered immediately, for that answer was, and remains, central to Judaism, being in many ways the lynchpin that holds all the rest together and gives it purpose inasmuch as without it, Judaism has neither consolation nor design.

Good Jew and irregular rabbi that he was, Jesus accepts that answer as the only one possible and counters with the only response possible. "If that be true," He says, "then how can it be that David, inspired by God himself, calls Messiah Lord? If David calls Messiah Master, how can Messiah be David's son?"

And there was, of course, no answer to that question. There never is to a mystery. There is no answer because an answer would only wither the elegance, the poetry, the awful beauty of faith and leave us merely human again, stripped bare of all that exceeds us, for in the end it is Dorothy's poem that holds the truth:

Lovely Lady dressed in blue
God was just your little Boy
And you know the way.
Lovely Lady dressed in blue
Teach us this Christmas Sunday
How to watch and pray.
Let us pray.

Purify our conscience, Almighty God, by your daily visitation, that your Son Jesus Christ at his coming may find in us a mansion prepared for Himself who lives and reigns with you in the unity of the Holy Spirit, one God, now and forever. Amen.

—first published as a Day 1 radio broadcast, December 22, 2002

* * *

Tickle's prayer roots run deep, as she communicates in all of her work. Her autobiography begins: "My father taught me to love words, and my mother taught me to pray." She continues to describe her mother's afternoon ritual of sitting down with her magazine, manicure kit, and Bible; after attending to all three in turn, "Just as the hall clock struck four, Mother closed the Bible, setting it, too, on the sofa's middle cushion. She turned off the lamp, she crossed her short legs at the ankles, and she went somewhere."[7] *That sense of "going somewhere" is one of the inspirations for what, in Tickle, became the observance of the ancient ritual of fixed-hour prayer.*

7. *The Shaping of a Life*, 3, 8.

The two pieces that follow flesh out the story of Tickle's involvement in fixed-hour prayer—first devotionally and personally; second, historically and theologically. This work, in all of those aspects, preoccupied her life and work for a decade. I am struck, in "My Part," by how often she uses the word "it" to refer to, well, it, which seems to signal that prayer is not only God's grace to us in relationship but our work—as well as a work in itself.

MY PART

The Divine Office is a set of prayers, almost always ones of praise, based on the Psalms, that is offered by many Christians at a fixed hour seven times a day. It is the work of God. It's the only work of God I know how to do. I do it five times a day.

I do this because we're told in Christianity that there must be constant prayer in our lives and also that there should be a constant cascade of prayer offered before the throne of God. On the appointed hour, in my time zone, I offer my daily Office for whatever time of day it is at that point, and when I finish that, I pass it on to my fellow Christians in the next time zone. It becomes continuous and uninterrupted. It's not petitionary, unlike much prayer. It doesn't ask for anything. It simply glorifies God and acknowledges him.

It's also a way, I think, of remembering who it is I'm not and how very little I matter.

Certainly it roots me. It makes me part of a much larger communion. It removes the individuality that is so much a problem for contemporary Christians. There is not individuality in the Divine Office. There's no inventing of prayers yourself. These are fixed prayers that have been used for thousands of years, so that you know that you are part of a continuous stream of the word of God. You enter it, swim in it, swim back out into your other life, and then you go back in three hours later.

I can't imagine not doing it. Can't imagine what life would be if I had to go more than three hours without approaching the throne of God.

Does it do something for me? Perhaps. But what it really does is give me something I can do for God. This is the context in which I am. This is what I understand the Christian life to be.

Discipline is growing a muscle. And this is discipline. It's the growing of the spiritual muscle. It's the discipline that allows you even to check out, sometimes, when you're in the middle of a meeting, for instance, or in the middle of a high-pressure conversation and that watch beeps.

I drop back, and I'm doing two things at once. It's a kind of schizophrenia. I'm praying. If I cannot get away from the physical situation, I'm praying and talking at the same time. So you never escape. Once you put that harness on in the morning at six o'clock, you never take it off 'til you lay it down at ten o'clock that night. It is there. And like every good workhorse, you know, you belong to the man who put the yoke on. And it is to be yoked. It is to be yoked to the chariot of God.

Keeping the offices—fixed-hour prayer—was originally a practice of all Christians in the first century. They all did this. They did it because they were Jews. And Jews were taught to do this. Every little town in the Roman empire had a forum bell. And it was the duty of the bell keeper to ring at six o'clock in the morning, which was the beginning of the working day; to ring at nine o'clock, which for us would be a coffee break, but for them meant that they could cool it for a while; at twelve o'clock, which was lunch and a siesta; and at three o'clock, when you went back to work; and at six o'clock, when you closed the shops. This was secular timing.

Well, the first thing you know, by the second century, fixed-hour prayer in the emerging Christian church has become six o'clock, nine o'clock, twelve o'clock, three o'clock. The nine o'clock hour is terce. It's the third hour. Twelve o'clock lunch is sext, the sixth hour, and three o'clock in the afternoon is none, the ninth hour. It's a great story of secular time taking on a whole new life as liturgical time.

There are many effects of the Divine Office, one of which, of course, is the constant awareness of the presence of God.

Regardless of how I perceive myself, and of the mistakes I make, and the evil that I see in myself—greed, lust, all of those things—I've still got this core. I've still got, in the middle of my day, in the middle of all of my consciousness, this one place that connects me with the divine that's there, that's solid, that says, "Are you distressed by all these things you are? Are you heart-broken about all these things you have just done? It's all right. Come here." When I'm standing in that one place that is the Divine Office, I know God's in his Heaven and that I'm part of that Heaven.

—original publication unknown, ca. 2001

* * *

A BRIEF HISTORY OF FIXED-HOUR PRAYER

The Age of the Apostles

Fixed-hour prayer, while it is, with the Eucharist, the oldest surviving form of Christian spirituality, actually had its origins in the Judaism out of which Christianity came. Centuries before the birth of Jesus of Nazareth, the Hebrew psalmist wrote that "Seven times a day do I praise you" (Ps. 119:164). Although scholars do not agree on the hours of early Judaism's set prayers (they were probably adjusted and readjusted many times), we do know that by the first century AD the ritual of daily prayer had assumed two characteristics that would travel down the millennia to us: The prayers had been set or fixed into something very close to their present-day schedule, and they had begun to assume something very close to their present-day intention.

By the beginning of the Common Era, Judaism and its adherents, already thoroughly accustomed to fixed hours for prayer, were scattered across the Roman empire. It was an empire whose efficiency and commerce depended in no small part upon the orderly and organized conduct of each business day. In the cities of the empire, the forum bell rang the beginning of that day at six o'clock each morning (prime or "first" hour); noted the day's progress by striking again at nine o'clock (terce or third hour); sounded the lunch break at noon (sext or sixth hour); called citizens back to work by striking at three o'clock (none or ninth hour); and closed the day's markets by sounding again at six o'clock in the afternoon (vespers or evening hour). Every part of daily life within Roman culture eventually came, to some greater or lesser extent, to be ordered by the ringing of the forum bells, including Jewish prayer and, by natural extension, Christian prayer as well.

The first detailed miracle of the apostolic Church, the healing of the lame man on the Temple steps by Saints Peter and John (Acts 3:1), occurred when and where it did because two devout Jews (who did not yet know they were Christians as such) were on their way to ninth-hour (three o'clock) prayers. Not many years later, one of the great defining events of Christianity—St. Peter's vision of the descending sheet filled with both clean and unclean animals—was to occur at noon on a rooftop because he had gone there to observe the sixth-hour prayers.

The directive Peter received during his noon devotion—i.e., to accept all that God had created as clean—was pivotal because it became the basis of the ecumenism that rapidly thereafter expanded Church fellowship beyond Jewry. Peter was on the roof, however, not by some accident of having been in that spot when the noon bell caught him, but by his own intention. In Joppa and far from Jerusalem and the Temple, Peter had sought out the solitude of his host's rooftop as a substitute site for keeping the appointed time of prayer.

Such readiness to accommodate circumstance was to become a characteristic of fixed-hour prayer. So too were some of the words Peter must have used. We know, for instance, that from its very earliest days, the Christian community incorporated the Psalms in their prayers (Acts 4:23–30); and the Psalter has remained as the living core of the daily offices ever since. Likewise, by c. 60 AD, the author of the first known manual of Christian practice, the Didache, was teaching the inclusion of the Lord's Prayer at least three times each day, a usage that was to expand quickly to include all the offices.

From the Apostles to the Early Fathers

As Christianity grew and, thanks to Peter's rooftop vision, as it spread, so too did the practice of formalized daily prayer. The process by which the fixed-hour prayers of the first century slowly recast themselves as the Divine Hours or Daily Offices of later Christians is blurred in some of its particulars, though we can attest to the approximate date and agency of many of them.

We know from their writings that by the second and third centuries the great Fathers of the Church—Clement (c. 150–215 AD), Origen (c. 185–254 AD), Tertullian (c. 160–225 AD), etc.—assumed as normative the observance of prayers in the morning and at night as well as the so-called little hours of terce, sext, and none . . . or in modern parlance nine a.m., noon, and three p.m. These daily prayers were often said or observed alone, though they could be offered by families or in small groups.

Regardless of whether or not the fixed-hour prayers were said alone or in community, however, they were never individualistic in nature. Rather, they employed the time-honored and time-polished prayers and recitations of the faith. Every Christian was to observe the prayers; none was empowered to create them.

Within the third century, the Desert Fathers, the earliest monastics of the Church, began to pursue the universal Christian desideratum of living out St. Paul's admonition to "pray without ceasing" (1 Thess. 5:17). To accomplish this, they devised the stratagem, within their communities, of having one group of monks pass the praying of an office on seamlessly to another group of monks waiting to commence the next office. The result was the introduction into Christian thinking of the concept of a continuous cascade of prayer before the throne of God. That concept was to remain into our own time as a realized grace for many, many Christians, both monastic and lay.

Christians today, wherever they practice the discipline of fixed-hour prayer, frequently find themselves filled with a conscious awareness that they are handing their worship, at its final "Amen," on to other Christians in the next time zone. Like relay runners passing a lighted torch, those who do the work of fixed-hour prayer do create thereby a continuous cascade of praise before the throne of God. To participate in such a regimen with such an awareness is to pray, as did the Desert Fathers, from within the spiritual community of shared texts as well as within the company of innumerable other Christians, unseen but present, who have preceded one across time or who, in time, will follow one.

From St. Benedict to the Middle Ages

Once the notion of unbroken and uninterrupted prayer had entered monastic practice, so too, almost by default, did much longer prayers enter there. Yet for all their lengthiness and growing complexity and cumbersomeness, the monks' fixed-hour prayers became normative for the religious in both the Eastern and the Western branches of the Church. By the fourth century, certainly, the principal characteristics of the daily offices as we know them today were plainly in place, and their organization would be more or less recognizable as such to us today.

Meanwhile for secular (i.e., nonmonastic) clergy and for the laity, the prayers appointed for the fixed hours were of necessity much, much shorter, often confined to something not unlike the brief minutes of present-day observance. There were also many public churches or basilicas that, despite their uncloistered nature, were pastored by monastic orders, and in these there was some, almost inevitable, blending of the two forms—i.e., of the cumbersome monastic and the far more economical lay practices. St. Benedict, for example, fashioned his famous Rule after the offices as they were observed by monastics in the open basilicas of Rome.

It was, of course, St. Benedict whose ordering of the prayers was to become a kind of master template against which all subsequent observance and structuring of the Divine Hours was to be tested. It was also Benedict who first said, "Orare est laborare, laborare est orare." "To pray is to work, to work is to pray." In so doing he gave form to another of the great, informing concepts of Christian spirituality—the inseparability of spiritual life from physical life. He also formalized the concept of "divine work."

"Office" as a word comes into modern usage from the Latin word opus, or "work." For most English speakers, it immediately connotes a place, rather than an activity. Yet those same speakers quite as naturally refer to professional functions—political ones, for example—as "offices," as in "He is running for office." Most of them readily refer to the voluntary giving up of the product of work as "offering" or "an offering." And those who govern or regulate work are routinely referred to as "officers" of a corporation or a civic unit. Thus in an earlier time that was much closer than we to the original possibilities of opus, it was entirely fitting that "office" should become the denominator for "the work of God."

For Benedict, as for many before him and almost all after him, fixed-hour prayer was and will always be opus dei, "the work of God," "the offices." As for the hours on whose striking the prayers are done, those belong to God and are, as a result, "divine." And the work is real, as fixed in its understanding of itself as it is in its timing.

Prayer is as variform as any other human activity. The Liturgy of the Hours, or the Divine Offices, is but one of those forms, yet it is the only one consistently referred to as "the work of God." The Divine Hours are prayers of praise offered as a sacrifice of thanksgiving and faith to God and as a sweet-smelling incense of the human soul before the throne of God. To offer them is to serve before that throne as part of the priesthood of all believers. It is to assume the "office" of attendant upon the Divine.

While the words and ordering of the prayers of the Divine Hours have changed and changed again over the centuries, that purpose and that characterization have remained constant. Other prayers may be petitionary or intercessory or valedictory or any number of other things, but the Liturgy of the Hours remains an act of offering—offering by the creature to the Creator. The fact that the creature grows strong and his or her faith more sinewy and efficacious as a result of keeping the hours is a by-product (albeit a desirable one) of that practice and not its purpose.

From the Middle Ages to Us

As the keeping of the hours grew in importance to become the organizing principle of both Christian spirituality and the Christian day, so too did the elaboration of the offices. By the eleventh century, saying an office required a veritable stack of books—a Psalter from which to sing the Psalms appointed for that day and hour, a lectionary from which to ascertain the appointed scripture reading, a sacred text from which to read the scripture thus discovered, a hymnal for singing, etc. As the growth of small communities took the laity away from the great cathedral centers where such tools and their ordering were available, it also created a need for some kind of unification of all the pieces and parts into a more manageable and more portable form. The result was the creation of a set of mnemonics, a kind of master list or, in Latin, breviarium, of how the fixed-hour prayers were to be observed and of the texts to be used.

From the less cumbersome listings of the breviarium, it was a short leap to incorporating into a book at least the first few words (and sometimes the whole) of all the texts required by the listing. This the officiants of the Papal Chapel did in the twelfth century, and the modern breviary was born. Breviaries, or manuals of prayer for keeping the daily offices, have varied over the subsequent centuries from order to order, from church to church, and from communion to communion within Christianity. So too has the ordering and number of the offices to be observed and even, in some cases, the setting of the appointed hours themselves.

The Anglican Communion, for example, as one of its first acts of defiance in the time of the Reformation, created a new prayer book to govern the thinking and the practice of Christians in the new Church of England. That manual was given the intentionally populist name of the Book of Common Prayer. More often referred to affectionately today simply as the BCP, the manual has gone through many updates and revisions that have adjusted its language and even its theology to changing times and sensibilities. Despite those changes, however, and perhaps as a result of them, the BCP still orders, through one edition or another, the spiritual and religious lives of millions of Christians, many of them not Anglican by profession and all save a few of them certainly not English.

As one of its more "reforming" amendments, the first and subsequent editions of the BCP reduced or collapsed the Daily Offices into only two obligatory observances—morning prayer and evensong. Almost 450 years later, in 1979, the U.S. (or Episcopal) Church bowed to the centuries and the yearning of many remembering hearts by restoring the noon office to its rightful place in the American BCP. In doing so, the Episcopal Church in the United States also acted within another abiding consistency of fixed-hour prayer—the enduring sense that the so-called little hours of terce, sext, and none, even when collapsed into one noontime observance, are as integral as are morning and evening prayer to the offices and to daily Christian practice, be it private or public.

Episcopal practice was not the first to undergo restructuring in the closing years of the twentieth century. In 1971 in accord with the directives of the Second Vatican Council, Pope Paul VI issued the Liturgy of the Hours, which modified the offices to an ordering very similar to the one the American BCP would assume eight years later. Four offices were now suggested to laity and required of monastics, secular clergy, and those under orders: a morning office called still by its Latin name of Lauds; a noon office that allows the individual Christian to choose the hour of his or her workday (either terce, sext, or none) in which to pray the office and, as a result of that first choice, which of the three possible texts will be prayed; the early evening office of vespers; and before retiring, the simple, consoling office of compline. Under Paul VI's rubrics, there is also an obligatory office of readings that may be observed at any time of the believer's day that is most convenient.

Despite all the diversity that centuries and evolving doctrine have laid upon them, the Divine Hours have nonetheless remained absolute in their adherence to certain principles that have become their definition. The Daily Offices and the manuals that effect them are, as a result of that defining constancy, dedicated: to the exercise of praise as the work of God and the core of the offices; to the informing concept of a cascade of prayer being lifted ceaselessly by Christians around the world; to the recognition for every observant of an exultant membership with other observants in a communion of saints across both time and space; to the centrality of the Psalms as the informing text of all the offices (a centrality made doubly intense by the fact that theirs are the words, rhythms, and understandings that Jesus of Nazareth himself used in his own devotions while on earth); to the establishment in every breviary or manual of a fixed cycle that provides for the reading of at least some portion of all save three of the Psalms in the Hebrew/Christian Psalter (the present manual employs a six-week cycle and some portion of every Psalm); to the necessity of fixed components like the Our Father; to the formal ordering of each office's conduct; and to the efficacy of the repetition of prayers, creeds, and sacred texts in spiritual growth and exercise. It is on these principles and within the scope of these purposes that the Divine Hours is built.

—from "An Introduction to This Manual," at the beginning of each of the three volumes of The Divine Hours.

Three years before these books were first published, in August 1997, Tickle had the experience of being "outed" in her fixed-hour prayer relationship with God in a television interview for PBS's Religion & Ethics Newsweekly. *Host Bob Abernathy asked his first question, seeking an answer to what it is like to pray the daily offices; then, as Tickle later wrote: "Instead of telling him, I began to weep . . . as one weeps when mourning. Something had just died for me, and while I could not name its name, I could feel its leaving." What had for so long been a private experience was suddenly, and soon to be widely, public.* Prayer Is a Place, 281.

* * *

Tickle's prayer commitments also run to the tradition-specific, as in this essay from the 1980s showing her warm affection (and humor) toward not only the nuts-and-bolts, but also the spiritual and organic power of organized faith as experienced in her native Episcopalianism.

HOW BEAUTIFUL UPON THE MOUNTAINS

Ember Days in the church year are dedicated to prayers for the clergy—to thanksgiving for them, to petitions for their increase, and to requests for their spiritual sustenance. Although historically the Ember Days were observed four times throughout the year, over the decades of the last century they have been most actively observed in the autumn.

As an omission or a diminishment of the liturgical calendar, the loss of the Ember Days never really troubled me much because they didn't signify anything that had been privately and emotionally important to me. But one year our church was without a pastor for ten months, and my appreciation and concern for our clergy deepened significantly during that period.

Most of us had never been without a pastor before. Midway through the months that we were unpastored, I took an informal poll after services one Sunday. I had to know if I were the only one in the place who found ours to be a distressing situation. I was relieved to discover that I was not alone—most of us had no idea of how to run a parish without a priest and absolutely no prior experience to draw on for help, especially not in a fairly small and fairly rural parish.

The usual and obvious things happened on schedule, of course. I mean that the lights were on, so apparently the junior warden was paying the bills. Bill Bains's elaborate spice garden and flowering borders continued to thrive in the churchyard. (They were oblivious to the need for any blessing except the ones that fell on them constantly from Bill's hands, I suppose.) There was always at least one service each Sunday, so either the senior warden or the bishop must not have forgotten that we existed.

I never did figure out who was doing our burying and our marrying because, selfishly but fortunately, neither we nor anyone I knew had occasion for either function. (Country parishes are rather healthy in the long run and not much given to hasty marriages. If my memory serves me correctly, however, the new priest performed three weddings in the first month after his arrival, but that is beside the point.) Baptisms we did on Sundays with the interim preacher of the day serving as officiant. Since baptisms are so poignant in and of themselves, I have always held that who the officiant is matters almost not at all.

But despite all the apparent routine and the surface tranquility, things began to change for us in those ten months. The size of the congregation dwindled more each Sunday, as did the size of the choir until it got down to a soloist for a Sunday or two toward the end of things. Since no one I know really goes to church to see the preacher, I found this diminution hard to explain. Yet I, too, felt its pull, its call to lie dormant because the parish felt dormant.

Holy days were not kept. For the first time in my adult life, day after day peeled off my kitchen calendar uncelebrated and unmarked save by private prayer at home. On Wednesday nights, the only church lights were the arc lights in the parking lot. Daily offices were unsaid. As a community, we fainted and were scattered abroad as sheep having no shepherd, a piece of scripture I never had appreciated until I watched it happening around me.

Then he came. Our new rector. "How beautiful upon the mountains the feet of them that bring glad tidings"—another piece of scripture that I never had really appreciated until I got to watch it happening around me.

It was gradual, you understand. No major events, no dancing in the parish hall. It was all very quiet and very subtle. The first thing I noticed actually was almost inconsequential. Grown men, all of them perfectly capable of having acted on their own without direction, suddenly decided one Saturday to spend the afternoon trimming the edges of the parking lot and poisoning the grass that over the past few months had broken its way into the asphalt in at least two dozen places. *Interesting*, I thought, *that none of us had seen it all summer or worried about it.*

The next thing I knew, there were people I had never seen before coming to Sunday services. Where he found them I may never know. And though I came to know many of them eventually, I couldn't imagine just outright asking someone, "Where were you when he found you?" much as I would have liked to.

Then the back row, and shortly after that the two back rows, began to fill up with babies, or with families with babies. If you sat anywhere in the back third of the nave, you were destined not to hear any single sermon in its entirety. You did gain, however, an overwhelming sense of our future as a body of God's faithful.

The next thing was that the holy days came back, not only the big ones we were accustomed to having but also the little ones that we weren't, the so-called lesser feasts and fasts. Six weeks into the new cleric, one of my friends in the altar guild sighed to me as we were leaving services one evening, "My goodness, he's going to church us to death!" I looked at her, and we both laughed out loud like those who have discovered water in the middle of a drought.

Or maybe I should say food in the middle of a famine. I had truly not realized how derelict we had become about the transient poor and homeless until the parish kitchen began once more to fill up with donations of canned goods. And I had forgotten how much I despised those tacky containers that sit on our supper table and say "Pennies for Hunger" until Rebecca triumphantly set one there and said, "See what we've got again!" It was fed more by her change and allowance than by anyone else among us, so great was her pleasure in once more having a priest to collect and use it. So the changed occurred, and we rejoiced.

I had occasion to drive to the cathedral one day and was greeted by the bishop as I went in the narthex door. In passing, he asked me how I liked our new rector, and I heard myself responding, "Just great, but it's a little like watching the Roto-Rooter man at work." He looked a bit nonplussed and I certainly felt it, but I knew I had said, albeit unthinkingly, exactly what I meant. Debris and obstacles and inertia just weren't there anymore.

My metaphor came back to me one day when I went to Morning Prayer and saw the hole in the back wall of our parish house. It certainly looked like a Roto-Rooter had hit it. In truth, it turned out that the vestry had approved the funds to expand the parish hall now instead of later; it appeared that we had outgrown the present one rather dramatically, and way ahead of previous projections.

Yes, Lord, I thought to myself, we do indeed have a new priest at our house. And that Ember Day it wasn't hard at all for me to pray for more of the same. How beautiful upon everything everywhere are the feet of them that bring good tidings; that publish peace; that say unto us, "Thy God reigneth!" Especially of Roto-Rooter men.

—*The Graces We Remember*, chapter 8

* * *

These final, brief statements about prayer come immediately after Tickle admits, "There are far too many words about prayer these days. It is as if, in our starving, we think a cookbook rather than a meal will feed us."

Prayer is a place.

Prayer is a nonlocative, nongeographic space that one enters at one's one peril, for it houses God during those few moments of one's presence there, and what is there will most surely change everything that comes into it.

Prayer . . . is the Tabernacle realized and the wayside chapel utilized.

Prayer . . . grips like home, until the heart belongs nowhere else. . . .

Prayer is dangerous and the entrance way to wholeness.

—*Prayer Is a Place*, 68

4

The Great Emergence

The Fundamentalist

Hands deep into the hole he's dug,
eyes half-lidded and April-drunk with sun,
he slides the trembling bulbs
down his thumb
into a wound he understands.

—*Selections*

* * *

It is important to realize that Phyllis Tickle was writing and speaking about the Great Emergence long before she wrote a book with that title. Several years before she published the book, she began to name the turn of the twenty-first century as a pivotal moment not unlike what was seen in the early sixteenth century in Europe or two thousand years ago in the Roman empire.

Tickle's work as a religion journalist in the 1990s paved the way for her trenchant analyses—always coupled with personal involvement—in what many others came to also understand as Emergence Christianity sometime around 2008, which at first didn't abbreviate but later came to be called simply Emergence in her writing around 2012.

We begin this chapter with an example of Tickle's analysis of, and enthusiasm for, the democratization of theological talk.

FOR THE LOVE OF THEOLOGY

Across all the old barriers of class and circumstance, cumulative literacy has provided readily accessible, expertly annotated facts and probable facts about both the objective and subjective world, facts that by their very nature impact constantly on the "big questions" that are God-talk in any era or culture.

Beyond the sheer, insistent flow of information that demands to be noticed, cumulative literacy has created its own kind of morality, or perhaps just its own kind of mass consumerist psychology. It has empowered ordinary people with unprecedented banks of information from which to draw down reasoned conclusions and with which to buttress decisions. But . . . by providing these tools cumulative literacy has also become a kind of imperative toward personal responsibility that has changed the roles of credentialed professionals and a popularly informed laity in almost every domain of life.

Once was the time when trained and usually certified professionals were responsible for the whole conduct of those facets of life that were thought to require art as well as craft—everything from law and medicine to religion, that is—but no longer. With such a wealth of new, newer, newest information, the lay man or woman feels compelled to re-credential every professional whom he or she meets or whose services must be engaged. The professional becomes, in this strange new paradigm, almost an artisan bidding for customers; the lay person becomes subtly but effectively a consumer "shopping," in our case here, for the best theology or soundest religion; the professional and the lay become codeterminers of conduct, credos, and decisions, with the lay person making the final choices and the professional, to a large extent, now becoming the worker bee who effects them.

. . . To speak of the democratization of theology is almost to imply that it is one thing, whereas in reality it is, like so much else in a mass-communications age, a construct, an effecting agent composed of several processes. The most pervasive subprocess is the mass dissemination of generic God-talk. Ironically, such standardization is the most visible component in our new mix, even to the most casual observer, while appearing to be the one most underappreciated by invested professionals. In fact, many, many teachings theologs and practicing clergy seem quite pleased to disparage and then summarily dismiss the standardization of the tenets of popular God-talk without serious regard for its implications. Few things, I suspect, could be more foolhardy, just as few could be more self-indulgent.

—from *God-Talk in America,* chapter 9

* * *

This article, like much of Tickle's best work, was originally given as a talk, and summarizes the themes that preoccupied her, and by her influence then, religious professionals all over North America before the turn of the twenty-first century.

TODAY'S CHURCH IN AMERICA

I have floated around *Publishers Weekly* for over ten years now. *Publishers Weekly* is the trade journal for the book industry. I do a lot of talking and working with booksellers, librarians, publishers, editors, and publicity people all within the book industry, which is essentially my purview. As I have become more and more concerned with my own writing, my job description has shifted, so, consequently, I also do a good deal of interfacing with the media. But basically my job as contributing editor in religion to *Publishers Weekly* is to interpret, to study American religion and, to some extent, Euro-American—because you can't really separate them right now—and try to analyze where it [religion] is and where it's going to go.

There is about a three-year lag between the idea and the book in your hand. It's my job to look at what we're doing, try to project where it's going to go and to take that message to publishers and say, "This is probably where the pew [parishioner] is. This is where the laity is. This is where the thinking is outside of the nave, but within this larger domain of religion in a secularized society. This is what you ought to be looking at."

It took me about three or four years at this job to figure out that that street works both ways. I can also say to clergy, "This is what's coming out of the publishing industry over the next couple of years. This is what's going to be read by the clergy. This is what's going to be read in the coffee shops in the field of religion. This is what you need to prepare your people to hear, receive and to incorporate into their own lives."

Then it spread from there to talking also to laity. For many, many years, in God-talk, books held primacy of place. That is to say, most of our God talk in this country and in this culture was done by reading books and then talking to each other about them. That's a little less true since 1999, when we got a shift, and primacy of place probably went over to television and movies. I date it in 1999, because that's the year the movie *The Matrix* came out. While it had many precursors in the movie business, *The Matrix* is the first movie where you could clearly say, "There is serious God-talk going on in this movie. This movie is wall-to-wall God-talk." It has an immediacy that the pulpit will never have, and an immediacy probably that a book will never have. Some of the same thing is also happening in television. A lot of it is happening in music. The book is clearly not the leader in what informs our popular thinking anymore.

Whatever else you want to say about Western Christianity or Western religion, you have to say that something is happening and already happened in the twentieth century that made a major pivotal change in who and what it is. At least twice before has there been a time when a culture so dramatically shifted that religion was dramatically changed also. The first time was the destruction of the Second Temple in Jerusalem in 70 AD. A bunch of irregular Jews who were followers of an irregular rabbi discovered that they could no longer function as Jews, that they were instead Christian. Absent the Temple and absent a rabbinical system that was not yet developed, they became Christian.

The second time we conveniently date as October 31, 1517, when a totally annoyed, totally irascible guy named Martin Luther tacked some thoughts on a door in Wittenberg. There had been prior to both those events a clear century in which all of the changes that those events conveniently date had come into place. If you had had my job in 1450, you could have been paid to look and say, "Oops, that's going to happen in 1517 or thereabouts."

I am paid to look at religion from a secular point of view. What I am as a Christian is a case study in organized schizophrenia—on Sundays and on my own time, I am the world's worst, most devout evangelical Episcopalian. I will persuade an apple tree why it ought to read the Book of Common Prayer. But during the week and when I'm working, I am paid to look at religion as it is commercially applied. That is a fairly interesting job description, it did not exist a hundred years ago. There aren't even many people who do what I do right now.

Much of what I'm going to say to you today and next Sunday is seen through the lens of the commercial application of religion. It does not necessarily take an Episcopal point of view. It asks that you look at the world of religion the way the media and especially the book industry in this country look at it, and that industry is both proactive and reactive. You need to remember that. No publisher that I know of is going to publish a book that he or she doesn't think is going to make money. It is to that extent reactive. It has to be. It has to react to what I think is going to happen in three years in the nave. But at the same time, who and what we are as religious people is framed by what we read, which is where the book industry is very active. It is proactive.

Most of the houses that are publishing religion today—commercial ones as well as religious ones: Doubleday, Simon and Schuster, and Putnam—most of those people have religion programs that are headed up by senior editors or junior publishers who are some of the most devout people I know. This is certainly true in the religion houses. But even in the commercial publishing houses there are men and women who say, "The pulpit isn't large enough. Only the bookstore is going to carry my message where I want it to go." They see it as a sacred vocation, minus ordination. So that's what the book industry is made up of and what we're about.

From the point of view of a commercially applied religion, religion is not exactly what you and I think of it when we're sitting in the nave. We in the office like to think of religion as a rope. It is a rope or a strand or a cable of meaning that has always stretched from the beginning of time. From the earliest known civilization, there has always been this need to arrive at the meaning of life. Life is essentially unsustainable if it's pointless. Without meaning, we cannot tolerate or sustain it. And so we look for meaning.

That cable of meaning—like every good cable—is composed of three strands that are woven together in order to give it its strength. One of those strands is spirituality. One of those strands is corporeality, by which we mean all the stuff of religion once it becomes religion—the building, clergy, canons, real estate, and budgets—all of that stuff that is the physical and organized presence of the religious practice. The third strand is morality. You can take any particular religion and see that it is a pursuit of meaning that can be broken down into those three categories.

This cable of meaning, like every good cable woven together of three strands, has a loosely knit sleeve that lines the casing of the cable and holds the three strands together. This sleeve is the "common imagination." The outer casing of the cable that holds everything together is called "story." As long as the story holds, the inner workings of the rope of meaning will bob along and anchor the boat, and everything will be fine.

When story gets pushed back—when story for some weird reason gets pulled away—then that loosely knit sleeve of imagination is exposed. We humans have a tendency to put our little fingers through the little holes and worry it to death. Then we stick that strand back in, pull out another one and worry it to death. Eventually we get the third one out and play with it, and then stick it back inside. In time we paste the [sleeve] common imagination back, smooth the story on and we go back to being happy for a long time.

If we view history from that perspective, here's how it might look. In 70 AD the story had a serious interruption—the Temple in Jerusalem was destroyed. What was never supposed to happen did. Once the story [casing] was pulled back, the sleeve of common imagination was exposed, and for the next two hundred years the Jews, the Christians, and the Gnostics played with the nature [the strands] of what that new religion was going to be. The same thing happened in 1450 to 1517 to 1600, and the same thing has just finished happening. We may still be in it, but I think we are now through. The work of the Reformation essentially ended about ten years ago, maybe five years ago. What started at Wittenberg was a progression of ideas that reached, or will reach their culmination sometime within your lifetime and mine.

Part of what happened was that the story [the cable] suffered serious attacks; this caused the twentieth century to be dedicated to the business of spirituality. Now I want to spend some time looking at the twentieth century, but, with your permission, I want to say that the twentieth century started in 1902 and ended in 2002 or thereabouts. In 1902, those of you who are in physical sciences will remember, a fellow named Albert Einstein joined the Swiss post office so that he could think and eat at the same time. He served as a postal clerk for nine of the most productive years in Western history. During this time he thought mostly, and I am sure probably misregistered some patents and sent some mail to the wrong places. (Since the man never learned to tie his shoes, I don't know why we'd think he'd learn to do anything else.)

Anyway, this is the century of science. It is the century of pure science, but it is also the century of applied science. They call the latter technology. Whatever else you want to say about it, this is the century, first and foremost, underlying everything else, in which we learned to mass communicate with each other. That is a direct result of science.

Science, as it came in and began to understand and explain life to us, also brought us the means for the democratization of information, in our case the democratization of theology. In the twentieth century, we will see the birth of "cheap." Radio will come, television will come and the Internet will come. According to Barna Research Institute, by 2010, fifty million of our fellow Americans will get their whole spiritual experience on the Internet. They will never go into a church campus. Fifty million of them will get their whole religious experience and community on the net.

You and I both know that in 2001, for two Sundays and odd days in between following 9/11, there was a sort of spike in church attendance. It never made it to the third Sunday. Every major website of spiritual implication crashed and burned out of sheer overload. Websites were flooded by people who needed to have spiritual community and had failed to find it in bricks and mortar. Others found it by leaving candles on public sidewalks, in the atrium of businesses, and along corridors. We lit candles, and we left teddy bears, and we mourned, and we prayed.

My husband Sam and I go in and out of New York frequently, and I'm always amazed at the number of people who are still lighting candles around Fulton Street, two years later. This experience of mass communication has affected religion more than anything else.

This century, with its mass communication, took away from the clergy the license to be the only God-talkers. Some of us are really pleased about that. I've got a bunch of publishers who are mighty pleased about that. But what it also does is it means there is no informed gatekeeper. There is no informed gatekeeper on the net. That's the danger. Most of the time, you don't have ordained people running websites. Suddenly it's anybody's game—whoever can talk the loudest and most persuasively is going to be heard. (It also helps if you've got megabucks to push your voice.)

Most people in my business—and there are really not a whole lot of us, maybe twenty-five or twenty-six of us—want to begin an overview of these hundred years in 1965. Being contrary I don't start there. I usually start in 1937. Being as it's Memphis, I'm going to start in 1906.

1906 matters for two reasons. It first mattered because a fellow named Albert Schweitzer publicly asked the questions: What if the Jesus of Nazareth is not the Christ of history? What if the Christ of history is not what Jesus of Nazareth was? You can read in his diaries that these thoughts frightened him so badly that he stayed in Africa the rest of his life, knowing that by giving, he could at least come near to the Jesus of Nazareth because he truly was not sure who the Christ of history was. We call this the pursuit for the historical Jesus.

Dr. Marcus Borg has worked in this field, as has John Dominic Crossan and John Shelby Spong; all three are wonderful, devout, and dedicated men. In many ways I would submit to you that Jack Spong is the last of the Reformation voices. What Martin Luther began, Jack Spong gives closure to. Both are such rationalists, that the mystery can't seep in.

Part of the conflict of the historical Jesus is that somehow in the Christ of history, we lost part of the mystery. We lost part of the mystery. We fell into five hundred years of severe rationalism.

Those five hundred years were washed away starting with Mr. Einstein who said, "There is something out there so much greater than what we can envision or ever know." Science has been, in many ways, where theology is now. Some of the best theologians I know are in the physical sciences because they recognize the mystery.

Another thing happened in 1906. There is a place called Azusa Street in Los Angeles. In 1906 it had a little stable on it that at one point had been a Methodist Church. The Methodist Church had moved out, and the horses had moved in, and then a black man named William Seymour came. His mama was named Phyllis. I always remember that. He came from Jackson, Mississippi. He'd gone west by way of Charles Parnham, and some of the so-called apostolic church people out in Kansas City. He'd gotten a case of passion for God, and he began preaching in Los Angeles on a front porch.

So many people came one Saturday night, the porch fell in, and they had to move to the stable. (I've always loved the fact that it was a stable at Azusa Street.) They cleared the horses out, and they moved in, and for three years, a fellow named William Seymour preached almost without stop, ten and twelve hours a day, seven days a week, to white, black, Asian (of whom there were very few at that point), to wealthy to poor to anybody who would come. He talked about the baptism of the Spirit and how at Pentecost, the Spirit had come, and [people there] had spoken in tongues, and they had filled the world with change, and by God, it could happen again. And it did in 1906. Suddenly, one evening on Azusa Street, the spirit fell, and the place was as filled as on the day of Pentecost with the speaking in tongues, with the fire of the Spirit, with every evidence of the charism of the Holy Ghost.

There was, sitting in that audience, a young man who had gone west because he was apostolic and because he heard they were praying for the Spirit and because he, too, believed it might happen, and his name was Charles Mason. We call him Bishop Mason. He came from Memphis, Tennessee. It was at Azusa Street that he received the Spirit. Some months after receiving the Spirit and the gift of tongues, he received sanctification. This is a step white culture does not normally recognize, but black culture does. In the business of sanctification you go beyond mere conversion, and you become, indeed, Christ's own.

That young man, Charles Mason, came back to Memphis, Tennessee, and he began to preach, and out of it came the Church of God in Christ. It is the eighth largest Christian church internationally. And it came from this.

Why it's important is that Azusa Street is the beginning of Pentecostalism. There had been a lot of holy rollers, but holy rollers aren't the same thing as Pentecostal. There are eyewitness records of this event in which people—street workers—were speaking German, Spanish, French, Italian, and even ancient Greek coherently. We're not talking about gobbledygook. Some of it would seem like gobbledygook. The gift of tongues was a substantial mark of the coming of something that has rippled through this whole century and rippled into our lives right now.

One of the things that Pentecostalism gives us is that sure knowledge that prayer works. It happened because these people prayed. It happened because they believed it was going to happen. It's what we've forgotten how to do, especially in the mainline churches. We've lost our zest for doing this kind of frank, outright pouring of emotion and dedication. It's with the fire. You see it now in the Toronto blessing. You see it in the Brownsville laughter. You see it all over the country. When you read those things, those are Pentecostals who are still on fire.

When we speak of this as the century of the Spirit, we have to say that the first time that the Spirit was hearing us and moving with us happened on Azusa Street. But there is in that, also, the sense of physicalness that religion had lost in this country—a sense of body and soul belonging to each other—physical manifestations of the Spirit.

In nineteenth-century America people couldn't decide what it was they wanted, but they knew they didn't want what they had. The nineteenth century sees the coming of Christian Science and Mary Baker Eddy. It is based on the premise that the soul and the body cannot be separated and that one belongs to the other. It is essentially another form of monotheism. The nineteenth century also gives us Mormonism, which is the fourth monotheism. It's the fourth of the Abrahamic faiths, and to treat it as anything else is ridiculous. That's exactly what it is. It is to Christianity as Christianity is to Judaism.

At the same time during the middle part of the nineteenth century, we've got Seventh Day Adventists. They were centered in Battle Creek, Michigan. Their great guru is a fellow named Kellogg. Dr. Kellogg, who was an M.D., began to experiment with baths and spirit and prayer and diet. He invented corn flakes and a bunch of other stuff that you eat. They were all playing with this idea of the body and soul belonging to each other.

Orientalism or spiritualism, what we would call the society of theosophy, is not indigenous to America. It came in from Russia, but it did affect us. 1902 and 1906 did not just happen in a vacuum. There's been a kind of pull into it. But it doesn't all coalesce. It doesn't become in-your-face important until you get to the twentieth century.

The reason I usually start with 1937 is that in 1937 we see the birth of an organization called Alcoholics Anonymous. Prior to 1937, if something wasn't right in your life, you could not afford to say so. You could not afford to say, "I robbed a bank," or "My kid is guilty of fraud," or "My daughter is pregnant out of wedlock," or "I have a drug problem." The society around you, on which you depended, would have condemned you as a sinner and not right with God, and would have distanced itself. This would have been the end of you. You would have been seen as absolutely damned, and so you kept all of that locked up. AA came along and said, "You know, it's all right to not be all right. We're all human. We all have our weaknesses. Let us get together over this weakness called alcohol and see if we can help each other."

It's the birth of the small-group movement. There were no small groups before 1937 in this country. It is the birth of that. It is the birth of the notion that sick people mutually afflicted can help each other more effectively and better than can hired, trained people. Take another body blow to the clergy. We don't go talk to the preacher about it, we talk to each other. One of the great ironies and amusements and wonderful things is that most AAs now meet in established churches, to which they dealt a body blow.

The other thing it does is, it says, "We can help each other. It's okay to not be all right. And we can help each other be better, and we can do it in small groups. But before you do it, you have to acknowledge that there is some higher power involved. You don't have to call it Jehovah. You don't have to call it Yahweh. You don't have to call it Brahman. You don't have to call it anything. But you have to acknowledge that the force is with you." It is the first time that American religion pays serious homage at the altar of generic God.

That's the beginning in popular thought of the possibility that all gods are just different names for the same thing. That's the beginning of the notion that perhaps Allah and Yahweh and Jehovah are just different names for the same concept. It is an important thing.

In 1959, what AA calls the big book or the blue book went on sale in bookstores for the first time. For the first time, you could go buy one without going to an AA meeting. That is the birth of the self-help movement. Ten years ago, we didn't have a religion editor at *Publishers Weekly*. We had a guy who did one page once a month, because religion didn't matter in adult publishing much at all. It was just a tiny blur. But over those thirty years, from 1959 to 1989, you can watch the increase in self-help sales. I've had bookstore seller after bookstore seller say to me, even in the early '90s, what they used to take to the pastor's study they bring here to me.

The bookstore owners say when a customer goes to the back left-hand corner and stays more than an hour, they've got a big problem, and they're cruising my books to see which one of the books is going to address their particular problem. They'll always come out of here with at least one, and sometimes two books. It was the beginning of religion publishing when that blue book went on sale. After that came Hazelden, and all of those movements. The shrieking and the hollering movement and all of that.

In 1965 we changed the immigration laws. It doesn't sound like it's significant, but it was very significant. At the close of the nineteenth century we were building a lot of railroads in this country, and those railroads were all being built by Chinese. Because Asians, as a culture (if one can generalize), are marvelously productive and beautifully disciplined, the American labor force demanded that we close our borders to all people of Asian descent. That happened back at the turn of the century. I don't know whether you're aware of it or not. We demanded that anybody of Asian descent be sent back. You could not come into this country. So for that period of time, there was no Asian influence in American culture. Even those who were here, many of them were deported back to China.

Then we hit three mid-century wars, all occurring in Asia. American boys, then later American girls, went into those wars, and they met folk who were very good folk. They were so good they married a bunch of them, and they brought them home, and they became Asian war brides, or they became Asian war husbands with Vietnam. There began to be a softening of that anti Asian feeling, so that in 1965, in response to a great deal of public sympathy for the Asian folk, we changed the rules and opened the borders. What happened? They flooded in. And thank God. I say it reverently. They flooded into Hollywood and the West Coast, because that's the coast that's nearest to Asia. But this meant they flooded in where the media was. They flooded in, bringing with them Buddhism, Hinduism, and a culture that was totally comfortable in talking about the world of the Spirit.

Buddhism is not a theistic faith. It's a nontheistic faith—only one branch, the Mahayana has a god that we would recognize as a god, but Theravada and the others do not. They are a system of conduct. They are a philosophy. They are a rope of meaning without a god figure. But they have enormous conversation with the interior world. So, with the flood of Asians, for the first time what has been a largely rural Protestant American experience, one that had no time or energy in its physicality for any kind of spiritual conversation, came face to face with the exclusive beauty, peace, and strength of people who comfortably talked about the world that is nongeographic, who recognize that the space that's not here is still very real, is still very there.

You can watch Buddhism begin from the West Coast and spread. How many movie stars do you remember from thirty years ago who converted to Buddhism, who carried out the message. It swept across the country. It didn't convert us all to Buddhism. I began to get these wonderful books about [for example] how to be a Buddhist Jew. My favorite was how to be a Christocentric Jewish Buddhist. It was a mishmash. But it was the beginning of our having a rhetoric, if you will, a lexicon, a grammar for talking with each other about what it is to have a spiritual life. It is a big part of why, once the rope had been cut open, we reached in and grabbed spirituality out and began to play first with it.

—first delivered at Calvary Episcopal Church,
Memphis, Tennessee, then published on Explorefaith.org,
both in January 2003

* * *

This passage from Greed, *written in the months after 9/11, demonstrates again how the spiritual writings of Tickle include more than what one might traditionally name "spiritual writing." Some of her most engaging and important work involves analysis of where we find ourselves, religiously and spiritually, old certainties fallen away, new questions most urgently felt, in the twenty-first century.*

WE LIVE IN A RUPTUROUS, CONFIGURING TIME

During the twentieth century and especially during its latter half, the West and most dramatically, America, passed through—indeed, is still passing through the end of—a time as rupturing, configuring, and informing for religion as was, for instance, either the Axial Age or the Reformation.

—from Albert Schweitzer's first agonized cry of protest in 1906 that the Christ of history just might not be the Jesus of first century Nazareth, to the descent of the Spirit upon the congregations gathering on Azusa Street in Los Angeles that same year;

—from the founding and rampant success of Alcoholics Anonymous in 1935 with its emphasis on self- or group-help and its reverencing of a higher, but not doctrinally specific power, to the archeology and caprices of fortune that would give us Nag Hammadi and Qumran with their variant texts of, and variant commentary upon, our accepted story;

—from the Second World War with its Holocaust horrors that sent thousands of Europe's brightest and most able Jews to live in the United States as welcome agents of victory and thereafter as appreciated and accepted fellow-citizens, to the change in 1965 of immigration laws that for the first time in decades allowed people of Asian descent (people, we must note, who for centuries had lived in the subjective and spiritual world as naturally as they had lived in the objective one) to come among us less-lately-come Americans, bringing with them their spiritual riches;

—from the discovery of antibiotics and the unprecedented advances in medicine's ability to miraculously heal, to the urbanization and mobility that ruptured the nuclear family;

—from the magnificent silence of the Big Bang and an explored outer space, to the postulates of chaos physics;

—from the rise of radio and inexpensive publishing to the establishment of the Internet that enfranchised popular culture and spawned the democratization of information.

From these and at least two dozen more equally dynamic shifts and pivotal points in Western culture have come the changed circumstances and perceptions that have unraveled and slipped back both the cable's casing and its lining, leaving twentieth-century Western culture to finger its way through the mesh and explore as it may the strands of meaning that had for decades lain strong, but dormant, there.

—*Greed*, 3–4

* * *

Continuing the theme, if you heard Phyllis Tickle lecture anytime between 2008 and 2013, when she specialized in illuminating the present with a prescient understanding of the recent past, you may recall some of this fascinating material.

LITURGY AND CULTURAL ENGAGEMENT

Ours indeed are strange times. To say otherwise would be naïve. It would also be a travesty; for though our times be strange, they are most wondrously so.

Every five hundred years, give or take a decade or two, the Church goes through a time of enormous rupture and upheaval which, at least in the words of Episcopalian Bishop Mark Dyer, resembles a giant rummage sale more than it does anything else. While the bishop's metaphor is undoubtedly intended as a witticism, it nonetheless contains a body of truth that is both historically correct and immediately pertinent. Five hundred years ago, Western Christianity was embroiled in the Great Reformation. Five hundred years prior to that, we were embroiled in the Great Schism. Five hundred years before that, we—or our forebears in the faith and culture—were deep into the throes of a failing world system and the battles of the Council of Chalcedon. [For us as Anglicans, it is more than passingly significant, of course, that this one led straight to Gregory the Great and his holy determination to "convert the Angles."] Five hundred years before Chalcedon, we passed through what is increasingly being referred to now as the Great Transformation, that time in which all of history groaned and birthed a whole new order and way of ordering.

Were we Jewish, an astute rabbi would probably note just here that five hundred years before the Great Transformation was the Babylonian Captivity and the end of First Temple Judaism and, moreover, that five hundred years before Babylon was the end of the Age of the Judges and the establishment of the royal dynasty out of which Messiah was to come. His or her conclusion would be, in other words, that what we are looking at is a Judeo-Christian phenomenon. A good sociologist might counter, however, by suggesting that what we are looking at is not a religious phenomenon exclusively, but rather that each rummage sale has been a full-spectrum, across-the-board cultural upheaval in which the religious component has been just that—a component. Both the rabbi and the sociologist would be correct.

Our semimillennial brouhahas always spring from, and involve, every part of human society from economics to domesticity, from systems of political organization to operative conceptualizations of reality. Inevitably, religion becomes the central means for interpreting the chaos of reformation, just as it becomes the obvious means for structuring a system of adaptations that will grant spiritual and psychological stability to whatever the new way of doing things is going to turn out to be.

As important as it is for us to understand that the Great Emergence—that being the name for the current rummage sale—is but yet another chapter in an ongoing saga, it is equally important for us as twenty-first-century Christians to understand that there are certain historical consistencies that appertain to these times of cataclysmic transition. In none of the previous periods of regrouping and reconfiguring has the dominant or operative form of Christianity been destroyed. It simply has lost hegemony and been forced to modify itself into accommodation with the world's new socio-cultural and political ways of being. In every reformation, as well, Christianity has grown both geographically and demographically. Additionally, whatever the new or emerging form of Church has turned out to be, it has without fail advanced the depth and breadth of the Church's theology just as surely as it has extended her reach.

All our reformations, likewise, have had one central question, and it is always the same question: Where now is our authority? For the Protestantism and reformers of the Great Reformation, the answer was Luther's cry of *sola scriptura, scriptura sola*. Their religious and spiritual offspring know now that such is no longer a satisfactory, or even a tenable, answer; and so as a culture and as members of a faith, we struggle to find a different one, one that will be both palatable to, and efficacious within, our time and place.

We do not yet have our solution, though around the world we are working on it, each in his or her own way, in his or her own context. And like those who have pioneered through previous "new" times, we are looking for our base of authority not only in what we can see lying about us, but also, and perhaps more earnestly, in the artifacts, the modi operandi and archives left to us by our forebears. We mine our way through the surviving evidences and forms of what once was and once sustained. This semimillennial searching of ours rests on human need, of course, more than upon deliberated or even perceived strategy. The propelling assumption is that present times are in chaotic distress, but that there once was a time—five or six hundred years ago, a thousand years ago, fifteen hundred years ago, somewhere back there—when things made sense and the world was predictable as well as hospitable. If only we could jump the last half millennium of gathering tsunami and return to one of those times of stasis and balance, we would once more find the key to balance and relative tranquility.

As every one of us knows when we are thinking instead of unconsciously reacting, it is incredibly silly, infantile even, to think that there has ever been a time in human history which was heaven on earth, a time that was drenched in good fellowship and logical operation. It is even sillier to think that, in the best of circumstances, we could return to it, but hope springs eternal; or perhaps just instinct does. Certainly in our present era of total tsunami, we have seen, for example, a rampant kind of pseudo- or faux- or neo-medievalism sweeping Western culture, presenting sometimes even in rather bizarre ways. The rise, and now the holding power, of Goth fashion and Goth lifestyles speak to this. So too do the startling sales figures of books like *The Da Vinci Code* which traffic less in literary value than in a popular hunger to know what it was and where it went astray, the "it" being coherence and cohesion in human affairs.

Popular television shows with names like *Joan of Arcadia*, can hardly be said to reference the contemporary, but rather the previous and earlier. Likewise in the world of television, the use of chanting-monk actors to sell products as diverse as popular soft drinks or name-brand copiers seeks to tap into the same stream. So of course does the heavily medieval or pseudomedieval tone employed in futuristic works of art like *Star Trek* or *Star Wars* or in magical ones like the Harry Potter series. The list goes on, but the point remains that we seek for the balance that we perceive as having once been. Or if there were indeed no balance in those inaccurately celebrated times, at least there were the tools for survival. Something there allowed us to get from then to now.

While it may be easy to observe with a raised eyebrow our inchoate mining of the past in order to better fashion the future, it would be historically and logically unwise to do so for very long. That is, there is much truth in the old adage that those who do not know history are destined to repeat it. There is also an inherent wisdom in the argument that it is by studying our elders that we discover how to live. This is true not only because we learn from them what not to do, but also and more powerfully because we discover in their patterns and values what we want and need to do. We find not only tools for our own survival, but also a stabilizing identity for ourselves as conveyors of cultural heritage.

The late American theologian Robert Webber was an astute observer and interpreter not only of theoretical theology, but also of practical theology as it was enacted in human lives and ordinary affairs. It was Webber who, in the 1970s, coined the phrase "ancient future" as a way to name the going-back-in-order-to-go-forward thrust of a Western culture already deep into the Great Emergence. Because he was a theologian, Webber focused his perceptions increasingly on the forms and streams of Christianity emerging out of the West's post-Reformation, post-modern, post-Protestant, postdenominational twentieth century. And long before anyone else really grasped the full implications of what he was saying, it was Webber who would quip that "The best I can tell, we are rapidly racing toward the third century." He was right, of course, especially in terms of religion. He was also more than right when he published a book, likewise in the mid-'70s, entitled *Evangelicals on the Canterbury Trail.*

It would not be inaccurate to say that almost no one at the time perceived just how prescient Webber really was. It is even possible that he himself did not realize the power with which evangelicalism would rush into the Great Emergence, bringing with it not only its significant numbers and passion, but also the entrenched, ravening hunger born of five hundred years of living and worshipping without liturgy and/or without liturgical connection to the prior fifteen hundred years of pre-Protestant Church. But whether Webber fully understood the ramifications of his own insights or not, it would indeed be Canterbury, not Rome, that fed the Great Emergence.

There are, as we know, four streams or tributaries that, in their conjunction, form the river that is Christianity. In diminishing numbers, they are Roman or Latin Catholicism, Protestantism, Anglicanism, and Orthodoxy. The Great Emergence is removed by a substantial cultural history from Orthodoxy. It is removed by five hundred years of indoctrination from Roman Catholicism. It is removed by thrust and intention and, if one may say so, protest, from Protestantism, which is too new to sate the Emergence's hunger anyway. The most available and only acceptable contact with what the Church is and has always been is, therefore, the last tributary still standing: Anglicanism, including the Anglo-Catholicism that is a relatively small but very informing part of it.

At a practical level, it matters almost not at all whether the adoption and adaptation of historic Anglicanism, either by groups or by individuals, expresses itself in overtly Anglican communities of worship and praxis or simply finds its expression in Anglimergent communities where the DNA of the Great Emergence incarnates in modifications of established Anglican liturgy. The end result is the same: Anglicanism is the stream from which our times and those contained within the next three or four centuries will drink long and deep.

While the recognition of such a phenomenon may at first be pleasing—and even chauvinistically gratifying to Anglicans, it does not come without a great price and a huge responsibility. The price is that of allowing a treasured way of discipline and worship to run free of established episcopal control and find its own way in the hands and lives of thousands who have not been so privileged and so programmed. The responsibility is to hand on and hand out our treasures, like it or not, to all comers, for the furtherance of the Kingdom of God. Easily said, painfully achieved. Yet there is in our Anglo-Catholic attic a veritable treasure trove not only of aesthetic and liturgical delights, but also of balms and disciplines and incarnational practices for the healing of all who may yearn to own them. And it is, of course, the incarnational that, in a field of many operative processes, is the one most sought after by the citizens of the Great Emergence.

To bring into one's body the signs, marks, and diurnal rhythms of one's religion is to form and direct one's innate, human potential for spirituality to some definition outside of the self and the self's experience or purposes. It is, in a sense, to offer constant hospitality to the divine, to furnish one's interior receptively, to grant one's inner being the gracious accoutrements of cleanliness and stability. To assume into one's self the spiritual disciplines of Christianity is also to perfuse the self with the music of common or shared story.

Anglicanism, as a tributary of Christianity, has always so organized its affairs as to be ever mindful of these truths and, as a result, has always been inherently incarnational. It has assumed from the first that a religion which costs nothing and bears no physical imprint upon the believer is not a religion, being instead little more than a social habit or a psychological panacea. That recognition and the premises derived from it are central to the borning theology of the Great Emergence, just as both are central to the desires and hungers of the Great Emergence's constituents.

Whether one dates Anglicanism from the first century CE or from the coming to Britain of Augustine, from the Synod of Whitby or from Henry VIII makes little practical difference on the street, though the niceties of it as a question may matter within the seminary or the academy. What matters at an effectual level and in relation to the Great Emergence, though, is that the most direct and primal way into initially occupying one's own interior and then dwelling in safety there is through music; and given that, what matters is that Celtic music has inherent in it a keening, atonal, rhythmic mystery that answers no questions. Rather, it celebrates the space between the inarticulate, but experiencing, consciousness and the suprahuman. It was, then, entirely predictable that some of the Great Emergence's earliest moves toward finding and pursuing ancient future ways of worship over the closing decades of the twentieth century would be an ardent, thirsty embrace of Celtic music and of its cousin, the music of Taize. All over the Western world, Christians and want-to-be Christians, seekers and even just shy hopers began attending Celtic masses and meditating with Taize music long before the century was over. The usually unmentioned or unremarked fact in this trend is that such masses and seasons of meditation occur more often in Anglican or Anglo-Catholic or Anglimergent naves than in any other.

Many an astute person has observed that where there is aesthetic integrity, there also is some concomitant "something" that is very close to righteousness, even in the mind and soul of an unbeliever. None of Christianity's member bodies understands this better than does the Anglican one. Music may take one into meditation and a spirit-filled house of the soul, but the soul requires as well a house beyond the parameters of its own skin. Or, to carry the metaphor more consistently, the soul yearns for a neighborhood beyond its own fence lines. We as Anglicans may jest about smells and bells, about passionately bequeathed prayer books and less than illuminating candles, about sneeze-evoking incense and cantankerous altar guilds consumed by a neurotic absorption with fair linen. We may jest, but we jest in self-deprecation, not sincerity. We jest as a way if not of congratulating ourselves, then certainly of bragging without offending; and well we should. What we have known and practiced for centuries, the Great Emergence is now either learning and borrowing from us, or learning and joining us in doing.

The Christian spirit, if it is to have formation beyond itself, must have formation in Christian community, a principle that makes the choice of which or what community a matter of overarching importance. The spirit likewise knows, or sometimes merely senses, its own deficiencies; it perceives and interprets its own hungers. Five hundred years of meetinghouses without altars, of homilies without pageantry, of prayers with bombast but little grandeur have left the spirit of the postmodern Christian hungering and thirsting; common sense and observation have led that same spirit to rest a while in Anglicanism and to feed there.

But to borrow the outward and deeply satisfying signs of a faith, even of a colorful, aesthetic, and acceptable one like Anglicanism, is not enough today. It never was, in fact. More is needed; for even if the spirit is fed, the body still must enter into the conversation. It must be shaped as a house is shaped to the tastes of its occupant, and not the other way around. The ancients knew this, and Christians of the Great Emergence are not so much rediscovering it as they are relearning how to appreciate it as an operative concept in their lives. They are returning to the ancient disciplines that came into Christianity from Judaism and that have continued to inform the Abrahamic faith and, in Christianity's case, especially the liturgical communions.

Tithing, fasting, and the sacred meal by whatever name, be it Eucharist or Communion or the Lord's Supper. Fixed-hour prayer, Sabbath-keeping, the observance of the liturgical calendar, and pilgrimage. The first three center around the space that is the human body—its goods and its appetites. The latter four govern or discipline time. The first of these ancient and incarnating disciplines to assume any kind of remarkable and broad presence in emergent practice was the rediscovery of fixed-hour prayer, or of the daily offices. Eschewing the Roman breviary, some early emergents turned instead to the much less freighted and much more familiar—culturally, if not personally—Book of Common Prayer. From those early adventurers and from the traction of their growing numbers came the burgeoning of non-Roman manuals that borrow heavily from the BCP and yet provide relatively accessible guides for observing the hours in company with the Church Universal. Some of those manuals have become commercial best sellers, in fact, so great has been the perceived and continuing need for them.

The rather broad return to the Daily Offices by Christians who were not liturgical by birth or heritage, but who were definitively emergent, led in the last century to a rather gentle but steady increase of interest in the BCP itself and to a new acceptance of "rote" prayer as being a means of connecting to a body of fellow Christians in other places and other times. The prayer book, in that stance, becomes not just a means of ordering worship, but also a means of transport.

But once one begins to dip into the Book of Common Prayer and/or to set one's foot inside an Anglican nave, one is inevitably nudged into the recognition that there is an ordering of time here that is neither secular nor physical. Probably no part of Anglicanism has had a more subtle but informing impact on the ordinary emerging Christian than that which the rediscovery of the liturgical calendar is presently having at a lay level. The cry of "Why were we never told this before?" is not only omnipresent, but it is also almost always raised with some greater or lesser degree of resentment and belligerence.

No small consequence of the rediscovery of the liturgical year has been, of course, a rediscovery of saints and martyrs as acceptable objects not only of conversation, but also of reverent consideration. What was it that once upon a distant time made a saint a saint or formed an early Church Father or sustained a martyr? Who were they, and why were they? And how can I/we find such force of Christian character as to inhabit time in their way? These are not only legitimate questions currently being asked by those barred by heritage from having previously had such conversation, but they are also the rallying cry of Christians who have discovered within themselves a hunger for heroes and heroines of the soul, a hunger that will not be assuaged by anything less than informed recognition of heritage.

The other, immediately visible consequence of dipping one's toe into Anglican prayer books and Anglican naves is a passionate appreciation for both the Sabbath and the sacred meal as beautiful things to be embraced with joyful hearts. There is inherent in Anglicanism, also, a kind of generosity that acknowledges the variousness of humanity and receives into itself with good humor the odd, the outré, sometimes even the somewhat aberrant. While one may regard such a stance as Christian hospitality, it has the feel of grace that deals more in compassion than in doctrine. In a time of upheaval when all things are in motion, such stability and predictability of acceptance make the previously unfamiliar very attractive.

All of this is to say in particular the same thing that Robert Webber once said in general, albeit with two significant adjustments. One is a matter of change in Webber's wording, and the other is an expansion in interpretation. It is not evangelicals who are on the Canterbury trail. Rather, it is a much larger company. It is the Christians of the Great Emergence who, in large part, are either on the Canterbury trail or are absorbing and reemploying the characteristics, spirituality, and practices of those who do so pilgrim.

As for interpretation, one must be careful to note that all of this should not be understood as some grand explosion of Anglicanism. It is not, nor is such a conclusion the message in all of this. No one of us can know just now—or for several decades, as far as that is concerned—just what emergent/emerging/emersion Christianity will finally mature into. The only sureties are that it will mature and that, as it does, Anglicanism will be the stream of Christian thought and heritage that will influence and inform it more deeply than will any other.

Pray God, then, that our long Anglican history of hospitality will indeed not desert us now and that we shall find the grace to welcome those who wish to come and to embrace and support, even to the point of self-sacrifice, those who wish simply to take.

—originally written as a contribution to *Ancient-Future Christian Spirituality: Exploring Fresh Expressions from a Sacramental Perspective*, ed. by Steven Croft, Ian Mobsby, and Stephanie Spellers (New York: Seabury Books, 2010).

* * *

Here are three essential selections from Tickle's landmark book The Great Emergence. *The first two complement others in this chapter; the third is an instance of Tickle's beguiling way of making a serious point by homespun analogy.*

LOOKING FOR THE REAL JESUS

We need to remind ourselves, before we go any further, that "scripture only and only scripture" really was, if not badly wounded, then certainly badly bruised, well before Einstein or Heisenberg ever came along. Their work would only reinforce and broaden an investigation already in progress.

At about the time this country was being established, a German theologian, Hermann Samuel Reimarus, first asked the question that would haunt the twentieth century far more than it ever haunted his own. Basically, what Reimarus asked himself and his colleagues was a deceptively simple question: What, he said, if Jesus of Nazareth and the Jesus of Western history and thought are not the same?

Although Reimarus eventually wrote a masterful treatise, *The Aims of Jesus and His Disciples*, to address the subject, neither his question nor his carefully considered responses unsettled many folk at the time, simply because they had little or no access to either Reimarus or his ideas. His basic question, however, would prove to be like the miseries in Pandora's box; once it had been articulated, there was no putting it back in the recesses of academic halls and moldering libraries ever again.

Most auspiciously, it would be asked in print again in 1901 by Albert Schweitzer in a book called *The Quest of the Historical Jesus*.

Schweitzer, unlike Reimarus, was a popular public figure, an organist of some international stature at that time, as well as a clergyman. He lived, as well, in the early twentieth century, when the beginnings of mass communication—cheap books, ubiquitous newspapers, a reliable and inexpensive postal service—made it harder to keep ideas contained, especially if they were a bit scandalous or insurrectionist. And Schweitzer's ideas were; for he concluded that Jesus of Nazareth was not the same entity as the Christ of Western Christianity and Western thought. He concluded as well that we could never know that "real" or historical Jesus. As a result of its huge, popular impact, Schweitzer's *Quest* is usually regarded now as marking the end of one era in *sola scriptura* and empowering the opening of another.

Some four decades later, before the midcentury, scholars would begin to theorize, using literary deconstruction and form criticism, just where and how editors or redactors had changed original texts into those we today recognize as the canonical Gospels. Others would work to physically discover and define the accumulating layers of text that undergird the editions we have. The discoveries of Nag Hammadi and Qumran in 1945 and 1947 respectively, along with more recent archaeological finds, would furnish primary sources in physical support of much of what earlier had been only theory. By the closing decades of the twentieth century, Jesus scholarship, with Reimarus, Schweitzer, and Heisenberg as its intellectual forebears, had become the life work, in public space, of superb and popularizing scholars like Marcus Borg, John Dominic Crossan, Elaine Pagels, and Karen King.

What their work in aggregate seemed to offer up to public view was a Jesus who was as much guru and sage as God Incarnate. In response, other, equally well-known and popularly published thinkers and researchers, working with the same tools and as various in background as Fr. Raymond E. Brown and

Rabbi Jacob Neusner or Bishop N. T. Wright, worked to lessen the subjectivity of Jesus scholarship by focusing on the Judaism in which He lived, contending that historical context is the soundest critical tool available to us for faithful exploration and discovery. Either way, Heisenberg, had he been alive in 2000, would undoubtedly have been amazed at just how much difference a little physics can make in a village church.

And though Einstein may have deplored Heisenberg's uncertainty principle and correctly foreseen, unlike Heisenberg, what the cultural and religious ramifications of it would most surely be, he too cannot be allowed to leave the scripture only—only scripture conversation scot-free. In 1915–16, Einstein published what was the last of his great papers, his "General Theory of Relativity."

Out of the mathematics of general relativity would come ideas and postulates that are themselves also matters now of household conversation: time as another, and fourth, dimension; time as capable of being slowed; the ongoing expansion of the universe; the Big Bang. And in conjunction with the work of other brilliant, popularly known physicists like Edwin Hubble, general relativity would eventually make it possible, on July 20, 1969, for Neil Armstrong and Buzz Aldrin to walk on the surface of Earth's moon. In doing so, they walked on what always before had been the footstool of God, and that made all the difference. Literalism based on inerrancy could not survive the blow (though it would die a slow and painful death); and without inerrancy-based literalism, the divine authority of scripture was decentralized, subject to the caprices of human interpretation, turned into some kind of pick-and-choose bazaar for skillful hagglers. Where now is our authority?

* * *

ENTER PENTECOSTALISM

But if 1905 had been an *annus mirabilis* (when Einstein first published his theory of relativity), 1906 could hardly be called a slouch either. In February of that year, a young black preacher named William Seymour left Kansas, headed toward Los Angeles and the call to come and preach his strange doctrine that baptism in the Holy Spirit was accompanied by the gift of speaking in tongues (both glossolalia and zenolalia). Within less than two weeks, the church that originally had invited Seymour to preach had barred their doors against him and his appalling doctrine, forcing him to move his sermonizing to the home of a supportive couple, Richard and Ruth Asberry. From the Asberrys' modest home on North Bonnie Brae Street in Los Angeles, Seymour preached to a small but growing crowd without incident or fanfare until April 9. That night, during the evening sermon, one of Seymour's listeners, Edward S. Lee, suddenly spoke in tongues for the first time. Three days later, Seymour himself received the gift, as did many of the others present.

Word of what was happening on North Bonnie Brae spread like a wildfire through the Latino and Negro communities of L.A. and, shockingly enough for those days, through Caucasian ones as well. The next night, so large a crowd of every race and social class and both genders gathered on the porch of the Asberry home that the porch itself collapsed, doing damage as well to the house's foundation. Two days later, on April 14, 1906, Seymour preached his first sermon in an old, cleaned-up and converted livery stable at 312 Azusa Street, and the rest is history. The rest is soul-changing, history-changing history, in fact; Pentecostalism would become a major player in the new rummage sale.

There had been a series of Pentecostal-like events before the Azusa Street revival. Some were as far away as Wales and Switzerland, and others as close as western North Carolina. Charles Parham, whose ministry was located in Kansas, for instance, was the one who originally had taught Seymour; and Parham is still regarded today as one of the founders of Pentecostalism. It is always Azusa Street, however, that is acknowledged as its true starting point. And over the next century, Pentecostalism, Azusa Street style, would sweep not only North America but the whole globe. By 2006, the number of Pentecostal and charismatic

Christians would exceed five hundred million, making them second only to Roman Catholicism as the world's largest Christian body.

Because Pentecostalism had its roots deep in egalitarianism, it was to come into North American Christian experience as the first visible fulfillment of the apostle's cry that "In Christ, we are all one body." Pentecostalism's demonstration of a Church of all classes and races and both genders became a kind of living proof text that first horrified, then unsettled, then convicted, and ultimately helped change congregational structure in the United States, regardless of denomination. In addition, the often loud, often apparently disorderly, always musical and participatory worship of the Pentecostal movement came in time to make the worship of the established Protestant denominations look as if they were somewhere between corseted and downright dead by boredom. Participatory worship became the standard, especially in evangelical Christianity, which is Pentecostalism's nearest kin in bloodline.

The impact of the African American experience on North American Christianity was and remains enormous. To begin even to sketch it requires a freestanding volume just on that subject alone, a largess we do not have, unfortunately. Suffice it here, then, simply to say that the Afro-American community in 1900 was, by and large, the only part of American Christianity that had an active, native, or "largely untheologized" community-accepted spirituality. One of the great gifts of Pentecostalism to the greater body of the whole Church was its origins in, and incorporation of, the African American spiritual experience. The efficacy of historic black spirituality and the immediacy of palpable contact with the divine which it enabled have been central to Pentecostalism since Azusa Street. It is almost undoubtedly this last component of Pentecostalism that has caused it, quite literally, to encompass the globe as well as change the ways and expectations of non-Pentecostal worshipers.

All that having been said, however, we must hasten to say that in terms of the Great Emergence as an event in religio-cultural history, there is an even greater point to be made here. Pentecostalism by definition assumes the direct contact of the believer with God and, by extension, the direct agency of the Holy Spirit as instructor and counselor and commander as well as comforter. As such and stated practically, Pentecostalism assumes that ultimate authority is experiential rather than canonical. This is *not* either to say or to imply that there is denial of the Holy Scriptures. It is to say, rather, that forced into a choice between what a believer thinks with his or her own mind to be said in the Holy Scripture and an apparently contradictory message from the Holy Spirit, many a Pentecostal must prayerfully, fearfully, humbly accept the more immediate authority of the received message. The same thing is true when the contradiction occurs between a received message and the words of a pastor or bishop. Pentecostalism, in other words, offered the Great Emergence its first solid, applied answer to the question of where now is our authority. Probably just slightly more than a quarter of emergent Christians and the emergent Church are Pentecostal by heritage or affinity, and they have brought with them into the new aggregate this s belief in the Holy Spirit as authority.

* * *

LEAVING GRANDMA IN THE REARVIEW MIRROR

Having come from so lofty a set of considerations as those about Pentecostalism, we need to look at something that appears far more mundane and less portentous, at least at first blush. That is, before we leave the early years of the twentieth century, we have to look at the automobile. It had been around for many years by the time 1900 arrived, especially in Europe where men like Karl Benz were making automotive history long before the average Americans ever even thought about driving one of the things. So it was not the automobile per se that would impact American Christianity. It was the Tin Lizzie, the Flivver, the Model T. Call it by whatever popular name you want, it came upon us in 1908, and it was affordable, reliable, easier than a horse and buggy to care for—and fun! America took to the roads and never looked back.

The car was a boon that, like a sharp knife, cut two ways, however. It freed Americans to roam at will, thereby loosening them from the physical ties that had bound earlier generations to one place, one piece of land, one township, one schoolhouse, and one community-owned consensual illusion, of which a large component was the community church. The affordable car enabled city dwelling in a way that had not been possible for many Americans in the past. It also provided, very early, the mechanism by which what had been the Sabbath became Sunday instead.

Family afternoons on Grandpa's front porch after Grandma's hearty Sabbath lunch gave way to spins out into the countryside with or without a Sunday picnic. Sabbath afternoons with one's kin gave way as well to carefully tabulated afternoon calls on friends who lived down the road a bit. Within a few decades, the Tin Lizzie and her offspring would so erode the Sabbath that Sunday would become the day for shopping, for mall visits, movies, and dozens of Little League games, not to mention a significant number of major league ones. Sunday evening services all but disappeared; and early Sunday morning ones (or Saturday evening ones) were invented in order to allow the faithful to get their Sabbath worship over and done with early enough so that there would still be some Sunday left to enjoy.

None of this is inherently either bad or good, so much as it just is. What we have is a set of cultural shifts that came about, in large measure, because of yet another piece of technology, in this case the automobile. What does matter, though, is that Reformation Christianity had rested for centuries on biblical literacy, the nuclear family, and the conserving effect of shared, multigenerational reading, theology, and worship. While we may, at first glance, scoff at Norman Rockwell's short, chubby, apron-clad, wispy-haired Grandmas serving feasts to multigenerational hordes, a second glance should tell us something else. When mid twentieth-century Caucasian Protestantism lost Rockwell's Grandmas, it lost a large part of itself.

It was Grandma, in general, who asked during each Sabbath lunch exactly what little Johnny had learned in Sunday School. And while Johnny might be forgiven for occasionally fluffing a question or two, his parents most surely would not, were it to be discovered that Johnny had not even been to Sunday School in the first place. It was Grandma as well who, by and large, rode herd on the preacher and his tendency toward fancy or newfangled sermons and imported theories of God. Grandma was, in essence, a brake—a formidable one, in fact—on social/cultural/theological change. And because she was and because she asked often and directly about the biblical instruction going on in her families' homes, she served as something somewhere between the archivist and the enforcer of Protestant codes and sheer Bible fact and story. When the Tin Lizzie took away her kingdom of influence, it was Protestantism more than Grandma that came untethered and was diminished. We should note as well that the redefinition of traditionally female roles across all the generations was, and still is, a principal contributor to the shredding of the cable and the exposing of its parts.

—*The Great Emergence*, 80–87

* * *

HYPHENATED EMERGENTS

[A Homily]

I am going to preach this morning. Actually, in all probability I will be preaching by the time you read this. I will not be away from home in some alien pulpit, though, but at home in my own parish and among those whom I love. I won't preach, of course, because I can't. What I will do is just talk. And what I will talk about is where I was last week.

Last week, I was in Seattle at Fremont Abbey, which is the home structure or base for the Church of the Apostles where an African American female friend and colleague of mine, Karen Ward, is abbess and where a significant portion of the Fremont area of Seattle seems to gather to do its worship or to do its socializing or maybe just to lick its wounds, regroup, and go forth into the world renewed. None of those exercises is a bad thing for a church or parish to be engaged in, and most assuredly none is a bad thing for the folk who are the beating heart of Fremont Abbey.

Fremont Abbey is an Anglimergent church. That is to say that what you and I and all our kind are living through right now is referred to as the Great Emergence; and like the Great Reformation of the sixteenth century or the Great Schism of the eleventh century or the time of Gregory the Great in the sixth century or the Great Transformation that happened at the change of the eras, this one of ours also marks a seismic shift in human affairs, both religious and secular. When scholars call this one we are in the Great Emergence, they do not exaggerate; for as was true with all its predecessors, out of it is coming a whole new definition of what it means to be human, of how society should be structured, of what constitutes the good life . . . even of what human life itself is and how it may be defined.

In this Great Emergence there are churches, movements, congregations that are frankly emergent. That is, they are completely new conceptualizations of what church is to be. There are, in other words, many congregations and gatherings that frankly are emergent away from, or emerging up out of, the traditional flow of church as we normally think of it; and they are a legitimate new form of Christianity as surely as, five hundred years ago, bodies protesting the dominance of Latin Catholicism were emerging and protesting and forming new bodies of the faithful and were legitimately Christian.

In all of this reshuffling and reconstituting, there are also other parishes, however, other churches and congregations that are moving to embrace emergent Christian thought while melding it with extant and/or historic expressions of the faith. They are known as the hyphenateds. They are the Presbymergents and Methomergents, the Luthermergents and the Baptimergents, the Submergents and the Anglimergents, etc. They fascinate me more even than do completely emergent congregations, because they seem to me to be engaged in the more difficult task of bringing to the party the best of two worlds, the ancient and the future. They are hyphenated, in other words, because they seek to meld the DNA and passion and postmodern theology of a new form of Christianity with the extant body and operative history of an established tradition. Among them all, none is so absorbing or compelling to me as are the Anglimergents, of whom there is no better example than the Church of the Apostles in Seattle.

Part of my joy in this and my sensitivity to it, undoubtedly, is that I am, for lo these many decades now, an Anglican through and through. Standing in the nave of the Church of the Apostles last Saturday night, I was reminded again of the richness and the glory of that singular and never-quite-domesticated or tamed position, especially as it is being translated into postmodern Christianity. I watched people of all classes and strata, abilities and dress styles, and all kinds of sexual or gender persuasions come together in a worship that used much of the order of service laid out in the Book of Common Prayer but somehow remained innocent of preconceptions while revealing itself as long on mercy, compassion, and adamant belief. The worship at COTA was blatantly dedicated to the premise that the Bible is one narrative, not two narratives in one set of covers and to the even more radical premise that Jesus, the Nazarene, actually meant what He said in everything that He said, including the fact that the promises of Holy Writ are fulfilled in Him and had better be acted upon by us.

What will I preach this morning? I won't. I'll simply say to those of us gathered in our Tennessee nave that the time has come to take heart. Now, in this time of reformation culturally and sociologically as well as religiously, our brothers and sisters in Christ all over this country and the globe are finding generous and merciful and grace-filled ways to exercise their faith and to include all peoples; and we can do no less. That is what I shall say, and I will begin the saying of it this morning by reading aloud a collection of words that I have heard many times before but never received until last week when I heard them proclaimed in the mixed beauty and aberrant, warm, but not quite familiar hospitality of anglimergence at its most powerful. The words are those of Isaiah, the prophet, who foretold Messiah's coming. They go like this:

> Thus says the Lord, Keep right judgment and do justice; for my salvation is near and soon to come, and my righteousness to be revealed.
>
> Blessed is the one who does this, and blessed is the one who lays hold of it, who observes the Sabbath and does not pollute it, and who keeps his or her hand from doing evil.
>
> Neither let the son or daughter of a stranger who has joined himself to the Lord, speak, saying, "The Lord has utterly separated me from his people." Neither let the eunuch say, "Behold, I am a dry tree."
>
> For thus says the Lord unto the eunuchs that keep my Sabbath and choose the things that please me and take hold of my covenant;
>
> Even unto them will I give in my house and within my walls a place and a name better than that of sons and daughters. I will give them an everlasting name that shall not be cut off.
>
> Also the sons and daughters of the strangers that join themselves to the Lord, to serve him and to love the name of the Lord and to be his servants, and everyone that keeps my Sabbath from polluting it, and takes hold of my covenant.

> Even them will I bring to my holy mountain, and make them joyful in my house of prayer; their offerings and sacrifices shall be accepted on my altar, for my house shall be called a house of prayer for all people. (Isaiah 56:1–7)
>
> May it soon be so everywhere and in all places. Amen.

originally published on Jim Wallis' "God's Politics" blog, *Sojourners*, September 7, 2008

* * *

To conclude the chapter, first a parable, then a prayer, about and for the Kingdom of God.

ONCE UPON A TIME THERE WAS A HOUSE

Once upon a time there was a house—

Anything that begins with such words as that usually carries with it the implicit promise that a tale is about to be told. "Once upon a time" rarely is a vehicle for conveying factual or objective truth. Rather we have learned to read it as the set piece that introduces a bit of folk entertainment which, in the end, will leave us with a bit of folk wisdom forever wrapped in a memorable tale. All well and good and as it should be.

On the other hand, when a professional religionist begins something by saying, "Once upon a time," there is the hesitant assumption that the forthcoming insight or wisdom will be less folk or common wisdom and more geared toward making some kind of moral point. And when a professional religionist begins something by saying, "Once upon a time there was a house," there is every reason to assume—especially if the religionist is a Christian—that we are about to revisit, whether we wish to or not, the parable of the two houses. One was built on a solid foundation of rock so that, when the storms came, it withstood their onslaught and remained standing. The other was built upon a foundation of sand and, when the storms came, crumbled under their onslaught and fell down. It is one of the better known of Jesus' parables and contains something very close to folk wisdom or common sense in addition to its theological ramifications.

Actually, a number of New Testament parables are common sense or folk wisdom tales, requiring not much depth of perception to understand and yet still wrapped in the memorable skin of story and entertainment—which fact is, I suspect, a good deal of the reason for our having a certain kind of laziness about extending them into our own time instead of leaving them as quaint, but still honored, artifacts of an earlier time. All of this came to mind for me three or four Sundays ago when the parable of the two houses was the New Testament reading for the congregation with whom I was worshipping at the time. I've been chewing on the matter ever since.

So—once upon a time, there was a house, whether on sand or rock, I cannot say; but let us assume that this house was securely positioned, at least for our purposes here. Now this house of ours had an occupant. Who, we don't know, but an occupant. That occupant has a family—a mate, children, a few pets, and an occasional visiting relative or friend who comes for a visit. Now the children are all worrisome and gratifying and demanding, as children are supposed to be. The mate is the beloved whom the occupant can hardly bear at times, though it is clear that each of them is really in the business of sculpting the other into something that more resembles half of a new personality than it does anything else. The pets all bounce around—or the dogs do, anyway. The cats prefer to sit on their haunches, tails curled under them, and wait to be asked about what should be done next. Some of the pets are quite dear at times and not so dear at others, but all are fed and housed with an affection which, unlike that extended to the children and the mate, is largely untainted by any sense of obligation or duty.

The house has all the appointments that one would expect. There are windows, well positioned not only to let in the light, but also to admit of good cross ventilation. There is an adequate electric system that also keeps the house well lit, warm enough and cool enough, and very functional. Likewise, the plumbing is in good balance with the needs of the house, though like all plumbing, it will occasionally suffer from overload and back up or will be the dumping place for more than it can handle and overflow. These are ongoing nuisances that cause the occupant only passing inconvenience, but rarely extended difficulty. There is the usual division of the house's rooms into those that are more or less public and those that are private and also, of course, those that are distinctly personal—or at least, from time to time and on a routine basis, their use is. There is, as we would expect, a lovely, warm, cheerful kitchen which transcends the categories and simply is communal space at all times. The occupant, being a good person, sees to the house and its maintenance responsibly, consulting experts from time to time, when that is necessary, and spending time and money, as well as energy, in seeing to the house's ongoing good health.

In all of this, it is very clear to all concerned that the occupant is not the electrical system, though neither the house not the occupant would scarcely be able to function without it. It is equally clear that the inviting, communal kitchen is not the occupant, nor are the attractively dressed windows nor the front porch and flowers beds that complement the house. The furnishings, all of them adequate and suited to their purposes, are not the occupant, even though they are used constantly for the comfort, sustenance, and betterment of the occupant. And certainly no one would ever think that the occupant was the stairways which went up and down, from basement to first floor to second floor to attic, or even from doorways to driveway and sidewalk and patio. The occupant is none of these things, in part, of course, because the occupant isn't a "thing" and therefore can never be one. It is true, however, that the occupant could not long survive without a house of some sort, be it this one we are speaking of or some other shelter.

But the house and the occupant do share one commonality: they both will someday cease to be. Both will pass away. The occupant, who was not the house, will die; and the house, who was not the occupant, will burn down or molder down or be torn down or undergo some other such ending. All will be gone. All the pieces and parts of our lovely story gone into dust and ashes. All of them gone as pieces, anyway. What is and always will be is what neither the house nor the occupant, as separate entities, ever was. What is and is ever to be is home—the joy-giving, rest-filled, and light-bearing presence within experience of the reality of "home." What is is the translation of the passing tangible into the eternal. What is is the fusing of occupant and house into one that is neither, but both together. What is is a story about an occupant and a house that, in truth, is parable about the Kingdom of God, as in "Thy Kingdom come, Thy will be done on earth as in Heaven." Or so it seems to me anyway.

—originally published on Jim Wallis' "God's Politics" blog, *Sojourners*, September 14, 2008

* * *

A PRAYER

Lord, Jesus Christ, Son of the Living God, have mercy on me, a sinner.

Put Your yoke on me and lead me on the narrow path and through the strait gate, and into Your kingdom; and grant that I may love the Lord, my God, with all my heart, all my mind, and all my strength, and my neighbor as myself.

Take from me every desire, habit, ambition, pretension, and distraction that would keep me from loving You perfectly and serving the Kingdom well.

Make me like that piece of fertile ground You spoke of where the rocks and stones have been cast aside, the thorns raked into the oven and the weeds pulled and thrown in after them, so that the seed falls, takes root and bears much fruit, some of it even an hundredfold.

May that mind and heart which were in You when You were here be also in me while I am here, and make me a living branch of the living Vine.

Take away from me my hard heart, my cold heart, and my stiff neck; and grant me instead a heart of living flesh that I may love.

Show me my sins, Lord, that I may see them, and confess them, and repent of them.

Grant me remission of them, as well as absolution.

I ask grace, and pray for the guidance, instruction, correction, shaping, forming, molding, sculpting of the Holy Spirit.

I beg for the protection, guardianship, communion, and constant comradeship of the Holy Spirit of God.

I ask for the infusion and the all-encompassing, all-embracing, total surround of the Holy Spirit.

Open me from the core out that this may be a life of praise and thanksgiving, obedience, charity, confessing witness, service, and humility.

Grant that I may be filled with the peace of God, the love of God, the fear of God, and the Kingdom of God, the ways, will, work, wisdom, and worship of God.

Grant me the knowledge of God, trust and faith now and forever.

Redeem my life and my husband's, O Lord, and renew all the component parts of them: our hearts, our minds, our bodies, our souls, our spirits, that our strength may mount up like an eagle in accord with Your purposes and those of the Kingdom. And may the words of our mouths and the thoughts of our hearts be always acceptable in Your sight, O Lord, our strength and our redeemer.

O God, with Whom all things are possible, save my soul, my spirit, and my life and those of my husband and our children and their families into Your Kingdom, here and hereafter, now and forever. [Here a listing by name of all the above.] Open our eyes that we may see and our ears that may hear, and grant that we may be converted and turn to You and be found worthy to stand with joy before the Son of God, in Whose most holy name I pray, even as He taught us and asking You to hear it as if it were coming from each and every one of us. [The Lord's Prayer.]

Bless my husband, O Lord, and be merciful to him. Grant that his sins may be forgiven and that he may be comforted. Fill us with discernment that we may spend everything You have allowed us to have charge of and everything that You have allowed us to become in accord with Your purposes and those of the Kingdom.

Make us better Christians, better mates, spouses and partners, better parents, grandparents, great-grandparents, parents-in-law, and godparents [with special prayers for our godsons], better citizens, friends, adult friends, counselors, congregants, co-congregants, and parishioners [with special prayers for specific needs].

Grant that neither of us may ever say, think, do, or act on anything about spirituality, sexuality, ecumenism, or interfaith relations that is not given to us to say at that time and place.

Show me how to think about and better understand the role and purpose of love, marriage, work, Church, prayer, and hospitality that I may more faithfully act in them and more wisely write and speak about them.

—previously unpublished

5

THE OLD, OLD STORY

Religion 101–102

Petros, that jolly old bonhoffer,
sitting haunched beside the sea,
never knew that I and Thou
would contemplate so existentially
The Cost of Mass Discipleship.
But then, poor buber, he never knew
that Van Buren would become
a U.S. precedent.
In the hallowed towns of Galilee,
only low-born farmers tilliched
and even the shackled galley slaves
could scarce be seen to neibur.
Poor old Petros, sitting on that rock,
watched a sea on which he'd walked
and never dreamed of distant things
so marvelous or so ecumenical.

—first published in *Front Street Trolley*,
Summer 1980, vol. 7, no. 2.

* * *

Tickle has returned throughout her career to the words of the Bible, to stories that formed her as a child, the teachings of Jesus, tales of redemption and forgiveness, and the human search for God in a distinctively Christian context. It is fitting that this be the last section of this book. Here we have her reflections on various portions and genres of scripture, selections from late work,

The Words of Jesus, *poems, and portions of other books that touch on this essential theme.*

One might say that this final chapter contains the creed of Phyllis Tickle, in that what is here is all about the Christian Bible, its characters, its Story, the Way. However, without all that preceded this chapter, one cannot grasp the breadth and scope of Tickle's religious imagination, nor her faith.

We begin with more philosophical reflections about how we encounter what is sacred, regardless of our religious tradition.

THE SACRED IS

The sacred is. Humanity has always known that, in whatever place and whatever time humanity has itself been. Humanity has also suspected—and philosophers have made their reputations by declaring—that the desideratum, or the thing desired, and the sacred were cocreated and cocreative. That is to say, in a kind of maddening circularity of illogic, that we desire what we desire and then label our desideratum as "good" or "sacred" because we desire it; but we are driven to ultimate desiring and to our expressions of it by the immutable and inescapable principles of the sacred itself.* Thus, the symbol and the symbolized are both the same and ineluctably dissimilar.

—*Re-Discovering the Sacred,* opening paragraph of chapter 6

* Religions, as well as philosophies, have historically allowed for this premise as well, meaning that it is not nearly so heretical as it may at first blush seem. The presentation most familiar to the average American Christian, for instance, is the "doctrine of progressive revelation" or some variant thereof. While hardly cocreative in our contemporary sense, the tenet does admit of maturation in the creature's ability to grasp the nature of the divine; that is, the ability of the creature to work reverentially within the limitations of a specific era and space without fear of redactionary judgment. Moreover, liturgical Christians receive the same tenet in their established prayers. Consider for example the following collect appointed for the thirteenth week after Pentecost in Saint John's Breviary: "Almighty and Everlasting God, grant unto us an increase of faith, hope and charity; *and that we may obtain what Thou dost promise, make us love that which Thou dost command. Amen*" (italics mine).

WHY ATHEISM CANNOT REPLACE RELIGION

Atheism is not a religion. Like a religion, it can offer community and common cause to its adherents. It can have a powerful and solid moral code and even, under cordial circumstances, may develop a body of oral and written material that is analogous to, or is a form of, wisdom literature. In all this, it resembles religion.

What atheism does not have is the architecture of mysteries. One might even argue that, to the extent that atheism lacks sacred story and narrative thrust, it also lacks transcendence and beauty, both of which are hallmarks of religion. Likewise, the perspective of atheism is caught within the created order, while that of religion, by definition, exceeds it.

It follows, then, that atheism cannot replace religion, though in a secular context it can often prove to be a gratifying alternative for those seeking the benison of moral choice and the comfort of a common cause.

—first appeared in the *New York Times*, January 22, 2013

* * *

Tickle's love for Holy Scripture is a constant in her writing. During her tenure at Publishers Weekly *she often expressed affection for the scriptures of each of the major traditions, but when she retired from journalism she focused more intently on the genres, verses, phrases, and meaning of the Bible—her first and real love.*

I WISH I'D KNOWN

Like every Christian-reared and -shaped American child of the early and mid-twentieth century, I knew the Bible long before I knew the world at large. I knew it conceptually and contextually—sixty-six books, the Word of God, period (i.e., no questions asked, end of discussion). I knew it pleasurably—great stories (many of them ones that we would not dare tell children today, of course, at least not without a lot of hemming and hawing and explaining of them down into dull rationality). I knew it experientially. "Don't do that! The Bible says thus and so." (I suspect much of what the Bible as Rule Book was quoted as saying in those days came as much from my mother as from the Good Book, but the message was clear in either case: There are rules and this is the place you find them.)

None of those ways of knowing is erroneous. I certainly do not regret for one minute having been shaped by all three of them. What I regret is the missing fourth piece. I wish I had known the Prophets.

Within the parameters of my rearing, the Prophets were presented, when they were mentioned at all, as sure evidence of an eternal, atemporal, and still unfolding story, but not as passionate and vibrant human beings. There may have been some good tales to tell about them—Elijah and his fiery ride to Heaven comes to mind or, better yet, Elisha's calling down she-bears to maul the forty-two little boys who were teasing him about his baldness. But laying aside the bizarre, I never, ever was introduced to them as more or less normal human beings who were on fire with love as opposed to being consumed with rancor.

It was not, then, until late in my years that I came to understand the Prophets as lovers. As ones who, knowing God more nearly and more clearly than most of our forebears did, spoke—and still speak—as often in poetry as in edict and rant. As ones who, even when ranting, nonetheless speak always in anthems as they sound out to us the hymns of salvation. As ones who, living eternally in Truth unfettered by time, know the temporal uses of metaphor and image and employ them well. To enter the Prophets is to enter God's greatest—indeed, perhaps God's only—cosmic cathedral . . . and that's what I wish I had known sooner so that I might have come here more often and, thus instructed, lived more wisely.

—originally written to accompany Isaiah 1:1
in *The Way Bible,* new edition (Tyndale)

* * *

This short essay shows Tickle at her indirect communicating best. Look carefully for the subtle ways that the lessons of life and death with animals on the farm reveal mysteries of faith, even the Annunciation to Mary. Also, take note of what Tickle finds in commiserating with Mary at that miraculous moment: not the all-too-familiar "Fiat," but rather her fear and confusion.

ON JUST SUCH A MORNING

There were no walls to experience, the farm inside me being always larger and freer than the one that lay waiting outside my kitchen window. I was my own window that morning, and I came to my prayers like Janus looking both ways—outward to where Nimrod the mighty cat stalked the patio in pursuit of a guinea chick he didn't really want, and inward to where a thousand equally casual deaths and near deaths had blended into acceptance and peace in the balance.

Dublin the rooster stood tall on the gatepost of the chicken yard. During the winter that had preceded us, he'd lost his comb to the bitter cold, having preferred the pain of frostbite to confinement in the henhouse. Now, crownless except for his scar of black and withered skin, he swayed from his perch more vigorously than he had when he was whole. This too I brought in to me, this regard for scars and purchase.

The early spring crowded around us—around Dublin and Nimrod and me. It waddled with the ducks crossing the greening yard toward the fowl lot and scurried with the guineas in their frantic discovery of the missing chick. It grew deeply and insistently up the kitchen window toward me, vining and budding as it came, but I would have none of it. I'd not be so easy a convert to merriment that morning. Too many beginning springs had seduced me before that one.

Beyond the fence line, Flash, the gelding, moved away from the mares to look across the yard, an immense air of tragedy pervading the whole of him. He stopped briefly to neigh toward the kitchen door, lowered his head to scratch his neck along the cedar railing, and moved on. He had no prayers standing between him and his ordinary habits—no interior pasture in which to feed—and I was glad for the simpleness of his purpose, the directness of his life. Mine was not so—certainly not that morning, when I walked two lands, the one that I housed, having been built of daily pieces from the one in which I was myself housed.

It must have been on just such a morning as this that the young Mary first was told, first knew that she stood between two worlds, and "was troubled at this saying" (Luke 1:29)—and across the intervening centuries I reached out to her fear and reverenced her confusion.

Below me on the patio Nimrod tried again for the chick, but this time the cock was there. It was over in less time than it took me to laugh—the cock on the cat, talons burying deep in fur, beak pecking hair and drawing blood, fur and feathers intertwined and racing across the patio and into the low-lying holly bushes, Nimrod scraped free of his burden by the low-lying prickles, and the guineas on patrol around the bed. Even Flash had turned back to watch, and Dublin, ever a gossip, crowed his delight from atop the henhouse roof.

It was all too much for me, and I was at last seduced. I went out into the farmyard, adding, as I went, its frolic to my prayers. Of these things, too, is worship made.

—*Wisdom in the Waiting*, chapter 6

* * *

Although a theologian herself, Tickle has never claimed the label, let alone the profession; this allowed her to write and speak at times in a way that a theologian wouldn't dare—as in this selection from her important book about the sayings of Jesus. Her perspective is in a sense old-fashioned, advocating for a certain naïveté in how we read and understand the words of Christ, and postmodern, wanting the community who understands to be as open and flexible as twenty-first-century systems theory.

WHAT JESUS' SAYINGS REALLY MEAN

Because the Beatitudes are indeed the most famous Sayings of Jesus, they are the ones most commonly subjected to popular as well as clerical dissection. . . . I had listened to preachers or Sunday-school teachers or credentialed commentators tear Luke from Matthew or Matthew from Luke and then try to attach some great doctrinal significance to there being two renditions of His words and two locales for their delivery.

At first, that remembering evoked in me the same kind of low-grade irritation I had been only half aware of for many years. What I had not previously realized, though, was that the low-grade irritation had apparently escalated into a major and very personal complaint. That is, I am not at all sure that talking about variants in the wordings of a Saying adds much to the soul's formation. I am very sure it takes something away, even if that something is only a sense of immediacy, perhaps even of intimacy. Consider, for instance, what would happen were one lover to stop caressing the other's face in order to discuss racial heritage, environmental conditions, and individual genetic and circumstantial backgrounds as determinants of human facial structure. Such an example, while it may seem extreme, is nonetheless very close to being an apt analogy for what I mean to convey. An intimacy has been interrupted, and a consummation delayed.

If anybody at all understands the danger, both professional and personal, that attaches to making such a statement as that in public and in print, it is I. At the very least I will be accused of naïveté and anti-intellectualism. Heavens, I could argue that case against myself with as much ease and wit as anybody else, religionist or theologian. Yes, it is naïve. Yes, it is anti-intellectual. Yes, I mean it nonetheless, or I mean something very close to it. We have become lost in a wilderness of scholarship that forgot to bring faith and humility along for the trek.

I do not know, or even think I know, what the Sayings of Jesus "mean" in some kind of global sense. I do know, especially now, what I think they mean, what I think Phyllis Tickle is being taught and told and given in and through them. I have few qualms about discussing the effect I find those words having on and in me. . . .

Beyond wanting to speak some of my own truths . . . there is something else I hope for even more. I hope . . . to overhear something of what others who worship Him have perceived and received through engaging the Sayings. . . . This hope comes not because I believe that any single one of us has any more of a handle on absolute truth than do the rest of us. Rather, it comes from knowing beyond all doubt that we Christians are a community on earth and in time. And in this era of rapid communication and vast, informal exchanges of information, what each of us receives, accepts, and rejects is filtered over and into the whole body of the community. The result—the Church that emerges and is emerging—is, to borrow contemporary terms, an ongoing, open-source, self-organizing network or system. That system may be naïve by traditional standards, but it is also alive, flexible, changing, growing, diverse, and egalitarian, all largely because it can never assume itself to be either finished or error-free. Employed prayerfully, its very lack of hierarchy can produce, and is already producing, a kind of fertile chaos along whose edges changes and vitality find a nurturing natural habitat. It goes without saying, of course, that it has always been the edges where Jesus and His words have likewise found theirs.

—*The Words of Jesus*, 8–11

* * *

Another essay on the teachings of Jesus, specifically Matthew 22—this one was first written for a devotional audience, and so is armed with practical application at the end.

RENDERING IN OUR TIMES

When our Gospel for today is studied nowadays, it is usually approached either symbolically or metaphorically. That is, in hearing these words we feel instinctively that there is much more here than the literal details of St. Matthew's story.

For example, our Lord, as we know, was tempted by Satan three times following his baptism by John in the River Jordan. St. Matthew records the story of those three awful tests in the fourth chapter of his Gospel. Scholars who analyze Scriptures for us analyze among other things the internal parallelisms that are a major characteristic of both Hebrew and Christian scripture. They say, for instance, that having been tempted three times by Satan, the established master of spiritual evil, our Lord, of necessity, also had to be tempted or tested three times by the human, professionally established leaders of religion in his day. In other words, it is no accident, the scholars say, that Matthew who tells the story of Satan's three tests in chapter 4, then tells in his twenty-second chapter the tale of all three of the rabbis' tests, including ours for today about rendering unto Caesar.

The rabbis' three test questions, or temptations to heresy as they are called, had to do with the rules of Judaism. That does not mean that the Pharisees' questions were superficial ones or that they dealt only with obviously legalistic issues. It also does not mean that all the established religionists of Jesus' times adhered to the absolute letter of the law only as a way to control the devout laity around them. None of these redactionistic, rather arrogant conclusions is necessarily true. Rather, I think we must assume that if the test questions posed to Jesus by the organized religion of His day were to have any real bite to them, the issues raised in them had to have been ones of real, personal, and urgent currency among the faithful. The questions of temptation by definition almost had to have been built around tenets of dogma that defined for faithful Jews the essence of godly allegiance and serious doctrine in late-Temple Judaism, and only a fool kicks over the traces of holy matters lightly, for to do so can mean death to the soul.

Of the three questions of religious temptation posed by the rabbis then, the first was ours this morning—the question of whether paying taxes with the proceeds of Jewish resources to a pagan ruler could be anything other than a recognition and acceptance of that ruler's power over Jewish loyalty and obedience. Was such knuckling under not a violation of the first commandment which says, "You shall have no other gods before me"? It is a serious question, and any answer to it would seem to have serious implications.

The second and third questions of the temptation toward heresy are raised by the Jewish clerics immediately after the one about Caesar and are recorded by Matthew in the eighteen verses which follow those we have just read. The second is about the truth or lack thereof of a resurrection. The clerics posit to him a woman who, in compliance with the tradition of the elders, married each of seven brothers, one after another, each of them dying before he could sire children by her. The question from a rabbinic point of view was, "If there is indeed a resurrection, then whose wife will this devout woman be in it?" The answer given by Jesus is a no-answer of sorts in that he tells his antagonists that in Heaven there is no marriage, and thus it is a piece of intellectual silliness that they're engaging in. Lest, however, anyone might miss the point, Jesus does add that of course there's a resurrection, for God, whom the clerics rightly acknowledge is the God of Abraham, Isaac, and Jacob, is most certainly not the God of the dead, but of the living, and, therefore, how silly to ask.

The third and final temptation question was the rabbis' challenge to Jesus to define which of the ten laws of Torah was the greatest. Again, instead of giving any kind of answer that was determined by the parameters of their question, Jesus gives his inquisitors his beautiful, and also often quoted, summary of the law: "Thou shall love the Lord thy God with all of thy heart and all thy soul and all thy mind and thy neighbor as thyself."

And thus ended the three temptations of religion by human leaders which, the scholars argue, parallel the three spiritual temptations by Satan in the desert. Now this approach to the reading of the three is, as I have said, primarily a symbolic one and puts our selection today in its appropriate and larger context.

The metaphorical way of addressing the issues raised here is used most frequently on temptation question number one, the one about Caesar. We are so accustomed to applying that metaphorical approach these days that almost without thinking, when with our ears we hear "Caesar" as in "Render unto Caesar," we with our minds really hear government, and when we hear with our ears "taxes," with our minds we really hear any kind of political stance a citizen can take with reference to government. But not only is that a broad leap forward from Jesus' time into our own, but it may be—in fact, I think is—a real narrowing of the range of Jesus' message and of Matthew's record.

There is in Judaism an apocryphal story which says that during the time of the Exodus, while the children of Israel were wandering in the Desert of Sinai, they began increasingly to wear Moses down with their incessant infractions of the law. As they wore Moses down, according to the story, so he too began to wear God down with his own complaints about the errors of his ragtag flock. The children were scuffling with each other in the camps. They were playing with dice, the women were quarreling over their tasks, the men were feasting before sundown on holy days. The list of infractions went on and on, growing each day longer as Moses came more and more often to the Tent of Meeting to protest to God the absolute impossibility of creating a righteous people out of such errant material. Finally, one day God had just plain had it. And there came a mighty voice out of the cloud of Presence, and the voice said, "Moses, Moses, do you really know what's wrong here?" "What, Lord?" Moses asked. "The problem," God answered, "the problem, Moses, is that you're just more religious than I am."

Now while we may find that story amusing, it is also, like most stories out of Jewish wisdom, a very insightful and, I would submit, a very holy one. It is also directly in line with what Jesus is saying to the Pharisees and through them to us: namely, that religion can often get in the way of holiness for the chosen people of God, because religion is what happens to understanding once it has been understood, whereas holiness is what spiritual imagination leads us to struggle to understand next. Not honoring the difference between the two can get in our way individually, and it can get in our way as groups and organized bodies of the faithful.

When the first question of temptation came from the Pharisees—the question that is our Scripture this morning—Jesus did as he was to do with all three of the temptation questions. He simply did not answer it in terms of how it was couched. Rather, as we have just read, he said, "If we are talking about the rectitude of an action, let me see the physical items that are involved in its execution; that is, if one pays tax to Caesar, with what does one pay it? With a denarius? Good, then let us look at the denarius." And taking one from the crowd, Jesus, we are told, holds it in his hand and says, "Now, look here and tell me, whose piece of metal this is. Tell me, whose face is on here? Whose motto? Whose mark? Caesar's, you say? Why, then, it would seem to me that if this is Caesar's piece of metal, it should be returned to Caesar."

That's a nice bit of logic, a clever way out of a conundrum, a piece of insight that left the crowd either dumbfounded or highly amused or, in some cases, probably both. What was the pivotal thing, however, is the rest of what Jesus said. For as with the story of the woman with seven husbands and the summarizing of the Law, it is not Jesus' escape from the jaws of religious literalism but his instruction in holiness that we should hear. Having exposed the lack of spiritual imagination in the Pharisees' test, our Lord pushes on to the business of holy discernment. "Render," he says to the crowd around Him, "Render unto Caesar what is Caesar's, because it is Caesar's, but render unto God what is God's because it is God's." The trick in this life, he says, is in remembering to ask of every single thing we encounter, "Whose substance are you? Whose image do you carry? Whose face? Whose motto? Whose slogan?"

If a thing is the stuff of Caesar, if it is Caesar whom a thing serves, and Caesar from whom the thing's power and the affairs of humankind directly emanates, then render it back to Caesar. If, on the other hand, the thing is the stuff of God, if it is God whom the event, the action, the decision, even the thought or word before us serves, and God from whom its power in the affairs of humankind directly emanates, then render it back to God. But even in the rehearing and rephrasing of Jesus' answer, we know in our souls that its application to our own lives is unendingly difficult. We know that discerning what is Caesar's from what is God's is not nearly so simple as it sounds. It most certainly is not so infrequent or so simple an exercise as it was when there was a coin ready at hand with the words and signs of ownership already printed on it and when Caesar was an alien power rather than being the vote we ourselves are about to cast or the public opinion poll we ourselves are about to answer. Rather, holy rendering is the kind of spiritual fray we in this country right now seem to have to enter with exquisite difficulty every single day of our lives.

As creatures who are both empowered citizens and Christians simultaneously, we spend a good deal of our thinking and of our political arguing every day on the very issues the Pharisees raised. Jesus, it appears from St. Matthew's Gospel, would have us do our rendering today first by asking the questions of whose image and whose slogan, and then second, do as he did in his dealing with all three of the temptation questions. Jesus appears to be telling us, just as God did Moses, that the danger to our souls in wrestling with these questions is not the questions themselves so much as it is in being afraid to employ spiritual imagination, in being confined to the questions and afraid to question them. It is here that we may let the trappings of holiness, the rules and customs and traditions we have expressed it in, become our holiness, and that finally is the sin here, for it asserts and demands, in the childish way of Moses in the Tent of Meeting, that God and the things of God must serve humankind and the needs of orderly human living. Not so, says our Gospel today, not so. Ask the question and then by prayer dare to imagine holy answers to holier questions.

Let us pray.

Almighty and everlasting God, in Christ you have revealed your glory among the nations. Preserve the works of your mercy that your Church throughout the world may persevere with steadfast faith in the confession of your name. Through Jesus Christ our Lord, who lives and reigns with you and the Holy Spirit, one God forever and ever. Amen.

—from Day1.org, first published October 20, 2002

* * *

A STUDY ON THE LORD'S PRAYER

Our Father, we—I and those, both seen and unseen, who join me in these words, and those others whom our love brings to this prayer by proxy—greet You as source, essence, and totality of life; and in the union of familial concern, we beseech Your all-powerful mercy upon us and all whom You have created.

Who art in Heaven, the One Who is in an Is-ness which we do not know and can not imagine, but which we suspect, in our moments of transport and meditation, of being everywhere and all-where beyond the capsule of our dimensions, of being the surrounding place of Light that defines our darkness, of being the final purpose that explains us.

Hallowed be Thy Name, which wraps the unnameable core into whose depths we fall when in prayer and with which our bereft and wretched consciousness always and everywhere seeks consummation.

Thy kingdom come both here and hereafter, both now and forever, which words we offer in petition both for our souls' sake and as an oath of fealty to Your Beauty.

Thy will be done on earth as it is in Heaven; for there are worlds of influence and affairs so much larger than both my small life and our many lives that we will die, Father, unless there are some safe havens for our spirits here on earth, some hostels of peace and pockets of obedience to restore and encourage us. And beyond that, Father, we have loved the world Your will has created; and we ask You, of Your great mercy, to redeem it both in Your Son and through our lives that it may grow before You into the creature of Your intention.

Give us this day our daily bread and grant us freedom from the faithless destruction of asking for more. Make us agents as well of sustenance for all those who, in whatever words, raise this same petition to You.

Forgive us our trespasses as we forgive those who trespass against us for Your grace only can free us from the Hell within time of the condemnation of each other, of rancor, and of resentment. Be merciful, Father, and free us from this most corrupting and corrosive curse of our kind. Cause us as well to see—but shield us from despair in our looking—our own hideous sins, lest we closet them out of sight and unconfessed in fear of one another.

Lead us not into temptation whether perceived or hidden, for only through Your gracious help can we escape it or, having fallen, be allowed to survive it. Keep us instead, beloved Father, constantly in passionate love with the harmony of Your Law, constantly seduced by the mystery of Your Word.

And deliver us from evil, both material and spiritual, that our lives, as well as our words, may praise You and we may come to rest at last within Your holy Name when Time is ended.

—first published on Explorefaith.org, 2004

* * *

SPEAKING IN GOD'S LANGUAGE

The year was 1604 CE. Elizabeth, the Great Queen, had died the year before and James, who had already ruled over Scotland for some thirty-seven years as James the Sixth, was now crowned as

James the First, King of England and Ireland as well as of Scotland. His first acts in that new and unifying role were, predictably enough, directed toward securing his position in the minds not only of his subjects, but also of the world at large.

Nothing in the realm of human affairs is ever entirely secure, of course, and James knew that. But he also knew that everything, be it temporal or otherwise, is better secured if it can be wrapped up definitively in divine authority and religious approval. To that end, in January 1604 and before he was even a full year into his new reign, James assembled the religious leaders of his day at Hampton Court and there authorized a new translation of the Bible.

The king was fairly directive about the whole thing. In particular, the new translation was not to have a plethora of marginal notes and commentary as did some of the earlier translations to which he so vigorously objected. Even more particularly, the newly crowned King of England, Scotland, and Ireland wanted no part of the kind of notes and commentary that infused the Geneva Bible, the New Testament portion of which had been published in 1557, with a strong odor of the egalitarian Calvinism to which any monarch in his or her right mind would object. No, for James, the year of Our Lord 1604 was a year for establishing and permanently girding up the principles of monarchy as governance by divine right, of Anglo-Saxon supremacy, and of political unity among a newly conjoined people. It was, after all, the Golden Age of all three of those things.

And it was a Golden Age in more ways than King James's determination to influence affairs with a sanctified fist. It was the Golden Age as well of literature and art and culture for his kingdoms. Especially of literature. Shakespeare would live for another dozen years, writing his plays and watching James's new Authorized Translation as it developed and then came into being. And John Milton, master poet and the other book-end of that Golden Age of letters, would be born before the new translation was finished and would live on for over half a century afterward, quoting it over and over again in works that still command our attention today.

Thus it was that the good King James's Bible was born in a time of multiple agendas, intricate statecraft, and great cultural flowering. The new Bible was to serve God and to celebrate, as well as convey, the Christian message. There never was—nor can there ever be!—any question about that. But likewise, by royal intention and without question, this first-ever Authorized Version of the Bible was also to celebrate and convey, in its presentations and choices of word and phrase equivalencies, the dignity and magnificence of the English monarchy, the English language, and the English way of being. It was to be a mighty tool that would meld the various peoples under James into a sanctified, compliant, and justly proud whole.

As history has shown, the Bible resulting from that multi-pronged thrust was to serve all of James's intentions well. It would also change Christianity for centuries, especially in those parts of the world where Latin or Western Christianity was the dominant expression of the faith. But arguably, it is the elegance of its language, rather than the perfection of its scholarship, that has carried the King James deeply into the hearts and familiar faith of millions of people. This is most especially true of the four canonical Gospels and the Book of the Acts of the Apostles, where the possibility for personal identification between reader and subject has been, and continues to be, greatest.

None of this means, of course, that the language of King James's translators has always been pristine or that some of its peccadilloes have been easy to ignore. One can scarcely read more than a chapter or two of the Gospels, for instance, without coming upon talk of "kings" and their kingdoms. Sometimes, in fact, the very repetition of those words becomes grating. This is especially disconcerting if one considers the fact that the Greek of the received text, i.e., *basileus*, could have been rendered just as aptly as "rulers, lords, noblemen, etc." and their *basileia* as "realms." James the First, however, was inordinately dedicated to the notion of the divine right of kings as such and by that name. His predilection became the informing one and, by proximity as well as association, the populace's conceptualization of

Jesus became more and more royal in the fully political sense of that word.

On the other hand, some of the consequences of both the King James's language and the immutability of the Authorized Version it created have proved to be both charming and at times almost winsome. Over the centuries since James, for example, some of our most arbitrary notions of acceptable English grammar and style have changed dramatically. Nowhere is this whole process more engaging than in the Gospels themselves. Today, commencing an English sentence with *And* is an error closely akin to committing a cardinal sin; yet the seven straight verses from Luke 4:11 to Luke 4:17 of the King James all begin that way. For that matter, so too do the ten consecutive ones from Luke 4:58 to Luke 4:67, with numerous lesser examples scattered throughout the Gospels. The result of that flowing, now folksy narrative style is not only a sense of leisurely telling, but a sense of Jesus as the consummate storyteller as storyteller. That is, He may have been telling stories to make a point, but He *is*, none the less, telling a story. And all the world loves a storyteller, sometimes without too much concern for the implications of the story being told.

Beyond all of this, there were also, of course, some outright errors committed in publishing the canonical Gospels, many of them simply amusing. A 1716 edition of the KJV, for example, records Jesus as having said not "go and sin no more" to the woman at the well, but rather, "sin on more," a significant and enticing difference, to say the least, and one that was quickly corrected in subsequent editions. But then, only a year later, the duly corrective 1717 edition itself records Our Lord as having told "The Parable of the Vinegar" instead of that of the Vineyard. This one was also corrected subsequently, but not without an untold number of jokes and wisecracks having been made in the meanwhile.

Some errors in the canonicals were a bit more serious. Luke 22:34, in the 1792 edition, for instance, named Philip, not Peter, as the one who denies his Lord three times. Moreover, and interestingly enough, a few of the original errors of 1611 have become so entrenched among us as to have morphed into a kind of sacred text unto themselves. As such, they are no longer subject to correction. Of necessity, then, some of those original errors-cum-truth must appear in this series, just as they will continue to appear in every legitimate rerelease of the KJV. In the case of the present volume, for example, Acts 7:45 follows in the tradition of the King James and differs from the *textus receptus* by having Jesus, rather than Joshua, carry the Tent of Testimony before the Children of Israel as they traveled from Sinai to the Promised Land.

All of these things and others like them, diverting as they individually may be, must also be seen in aggregate. They must be seen, not as singular matters worthy of passing note, but rather as things which, in their sum, became the real significance of the King James for Christianity and, ultimately, the world. That is, by far the greatest impact or consequence of the KJV was the shift in the popular operative conceptualization of Jesus that followed its creation and use.

As British influence spread and Britannia came more and more to rule the world as well as the waves, so too spread the influence and dominance of the Authorized Version of the Bible which those things carried with them. Over time, Jesus ceased to be a short, Semitic peasant and became, instead, a tall, blond Caucasian of fluid tongue and nuanced elegance. He ceased, in other words, to be one of the oppressed, to be that long-promised one whose hallmark would be that he was despised and rejected of men. Instead, the KJV Jesus had the linguistic eloquence and cadences of those who ruled, who were the empowered, who were as we ourselves would all want to be.

It is certainly not difficult to understand how such a "savior" might be less than immediately appealing to those who had not been born English and/or were, moreover, being conquered and victimized by those of us who were. That one, as facts go, is more or less self-evident. What is not so immediately evident is how serving a privileged Jesus—one more or less just like us and who certainly spoke like the best of us—could turn Him into a friend and divine neighbor, how it could shorten the distance between radical obedience and camaraderie, how it could wash over into divine validation for us as we are.

We Christians who speak English today, either by right of birth or by acquisition, have been engaged for some several decades now in trying to release Jesus of Nazareth from that carapace. Even as we have done so, however, we have come as well to love the King James Bible, and especially its rendering of our Gospels, in a different and perhaps even more ardent way than did James and his coterie of translators.

The thousands and thousands of fathers and mothers who have gone before us in the faith since the seventeenth century are no longer the whole body of what we as Church are, just as King James's Authorized Bible is no longer the whole body of our sacred text. But like the treasured portraits and constantly revisited stories of those spiritual and ecclesial ancestors of ours, the King James, and especially its voicing of Our Lord in its rendering of the Gospel, are our history, our record of where we are and of the long, slow way of our becoming—which means that we can say to all who enter here, whether Christian or not, "Welcome not only to one of the world's most sacred treasures, but welcome also to our souls' home."

—original publication unknown, written ca. 2000

* * *

A longtime advocate and scholar of interfaith understanding, Tickle also entered life—and will leave it—a passionate, committed Christian. She understands that a religious tradition only "works" when one is fully immersed in its story and symbols.

THE NAKEDNESS OF EASTER

Easter is the straight stuff, straight, hard-core Christianity.

We can all enjoy Christmas because commercialization and secular culture have given it a kind of spiritual distance for many of us. We have managed, in this world of many faiths and careless tolerations, to agree on a Lupercalia or Saturnalia in which we celebrate and exercise that which is most intellectually acceptable to our common definition of what humankind at its best should be. In proclaiming universal love and possible peace to each other for a few hours of the midwinter, we absolve ourselves of the burden of hopelessness and perhaps of incipient godlessness, for Christmas can be shared by Christian, semi-Christian, and flagrant pagan alike, all of us agreeing in its moral stances and cultural postures. Thank God we have such a day once a year.

But Easter is not so tractable. It is not about morality and the common good. It cannot be shared with a Muslim fellow or a Jewish neighbor or a quasi-Christian. Nor can one write about Easter with the philosophical insights and enlightened self-interest of the professional moralist. Easter strips all of that away, and one is left naked of abilities, cleverness, and dignity. One is left, ultimately, with Easter. There is the mystery of eating this God, of incorporating him into oneself, body into body—a mystery so dark as to lie beyond the memory of humankind and beyond the reach of human poetry.

—from the epilogue of *Wisdom in the Waiting*

* * *

Here again is that deep affection for Judaism often in Tickle's writing. The Jewishness of Christianity is central to her understanding of the "Old, Old Story." It is also central to some projects she has planned for the future.

THE RUGGED GRANDEUR OF JESUS

There are no accidents with Jesus' Sayings, only a kind of rugged grandeur. There may have been—undoubtedly were—some textural corruption along the way, some paraphrase, some editing; but none of that has managed to distort or obliterate the themes. Once the patterns are excavated, the debris dusting their surfaces is only debris. And Jewishness is a major pattern in the Sayings—Jewishness not as a genetic construct but as a prophetic one; Jewishness as a divinely appointed and ordained human road into space/time for the purpose of completing creation. It took me a while to perceive the presence of that telling difference in what He was saying and doing.

People as living souls are all *imago dei*, but not all people and tribes have the narrative, the divine plan, the *institutum dei*, the intention of God. Only to the tribe of Abraham, Isaac, and Jacob has its maintenance been given; and of all narratives, it is the most particular. Fixed like a beamed bridge through time, it may suffer accidents and endure collateral abuse, but it cannot be destroyed. It runs from before Eden to the other side of Apocalypse and is the King's Highway, carrying on itself the caravan of God. And the last obstacle to be tunneled through was, ironically, the embroidered fabric of a Temple curtain. With His cry of "It is finished!" the veil that separated the sacred area of the Temple from the Holy of Holies rips from top to bottom. There is no more curtain between God and humankind.

—*The Words of Jesus,* 48–49

* * *

This brief essay is the work of a sociologist of religion who is also a person with faith, seeking to comprehend what it all means.

THE NECROPOLIS AT OUR HOUSE

The church has always taught the doctrine of the communion of saints—the principle that there is an unbroken union of all saints, whether in this world or out of it; that that community is inviolate; that it is a communion beyond the reach of mutability. Exactly what is the relationship between the faithful dead and the faithful living has been debated for centuries, but almost no branch of the faith questions the notion that there is a relationship. And almost every branch has been amazingly content to let the believer treat the problem in the way most comfortable to that individual as long as he or she didn't get too outspoken or too definitive in any opinions.

However the individual may wish to deal with the dead and/ or the ongoing communion of the saints, the church still holds All Saints' as a major feast day and still demands of us as believers some consideration of the question of death itself and of those who have passed into it.

At the foot of the pasture, just where the fence meets the bog, there is a homemade stile fashioned years ago of stones and logs by little Tickles seeking easier access to the village cemetery beyond our property line. Although it is not beautiful, it has, as contrivances go, been remarkably effective, having carried more than its fair share of cousins, playmates, and siblings across the fence from pasture games to graveyard play. There was a time when even the older children could recite the names and histories of at least three dozen of the cemetery's dead, so great was their intimacy with the place.

They played originally, of course, without any reverence and, as very young children, without any acquired regard for spooks and goblins. The cemetery was simply another part of our part of the village where another set of neighbors existed—statically perhaps, but existed.

It used to fascinate me that the children always spoke of the buried in the present tense.

"The General's got some kind of awful, red gooey stuff growing up his stone. John tried to scrape it off, but it wouldn't come. What do you reckon it is?"

"Miss Pink's flowers are dead. Do you think she'd like some of our marigolds?"

"Sam was cracking walnuts on Mrs. Todd's foot marker, but I told him to stop. She wouldn't like it a bit if she could see the mess he's made!"

And then, as each started to school and began to realize the broadening social world that makes school tolerable for most of us, I was equally fascinated to watch each of them tie their new friends backward, so to speak, to their dead ones.

"I met a new kid today—name's Jimmy Brandon. His granddaddy's over there under that last oak by the corner of the fence."

As the children grew older, they played less raucously in the cemetery, as they did everywhere else, of course. Each briefly went through a Halloween phase of wanting earnestly to believe in scary places and of wanting our cemetery to perform that service for them. But as a thriller, it was a washout. After all their years of playing and daydreaming there, the place was too comfortable, too familiar to make their blood race or their eyes see what was not there. So now it matters almost not at all to any of them except as a storybook matters: loved in childhood but outgrown in adolescence, it still matters, still instructs, still is part of what the adult becomes.

When she was home one autumn for a visit, Laura went down to see about it. At first I didn't know where she had gone until Becca, who knew everything, said, "She's gone to see the General. I saw her climbing over the stile."

When she got back, I was cooking lunch. "How was he?" I asked as she came in.

She grinned, a little sheepishly maybe, but her eyes twinkled as she answered. "Just fine, I think. At least he didn't complain." And then, in typical Laura fashion, she added, "And I did remember to ask him."

Despite such occasional visits, though, so badly built a stile would in the normal course of things have grown grassier and grassier each summer over the years. It would, in the normal course of things, have sunk lower and lower with the rains of each fall until it completely reverted to the rubble and lumber from which it came. But then grandchildren began coming along, still too little to haul logs and rocks or even to shift those that have already been hauled. As a first social experience with the dead, however, the old stile has certainly remained a comfortable one, and for that reason alone, it probably deserves more loyalty from us than most stiles do. At least that's what Sam Sr. said one day when he came back in from restacking it. Actually what he said was, "Why knock a good thing when you've got it?" but I think it means the same thing.

—*The Graces We Remember*, chapter 12

* * *

A fitting place to end. Tickle's writing often seems to begin and end with spiritual ruminations informed by philosophy, and often science—but always reflect back on what she has been given.

WHAT MAKES A SACRED STORY "SACRED"?

If we can see ourselves—and now we must—as more than intellect or awareness, and since we experience ourselves as something more than soul, we have come—or appear certainly to be coming again—to mystery. To the inscrutable. To spirit. Spirit, inextricably part and parcel of body and soul and bound to them. Spirit, the complementary third and compelling portion of our self, and the final part of our totality. Spirit.

Even the mind boggles before spirit's greater greatness and toward the hope its presence brings. Yet spirit, while it may indeed know itself (or so the ancients teach us), cannot be known to mind. Spirit elects, in fact, to deny itself to mind as does the cloud deny itself to the sea, though both are water and equally agents of it. Spirit projects itself instead like a cloud darkling upon the surfaces of the sea. And we say, being sea, that we bear the image of the cloud but are not it.

It is mystery. . . . We touch its possibility and are guaranteed in a way that exceeds even the comfort we gain in exercising soul. God in the thunder, God in the whisper, God in half-caught image.

. . . Humanity's sacred stories are sacred, the faithful would say, because they are true. I certainly am not inclined to challenge that position, but I do want to offer a more pragmatic addendum. Sacred stories are also sacred because they have survived; and central to that process, they have survived by suffering evolution. That is to say that by shedding what was irrelevant and retaining what was sustaining, sacred story arrives, almost by default, at what is valid. Moreover, the sacred story of America's three religions is, right up until the axial age, the same core story. The potential impact of that one fact—that is, the presence within one avidly seeking culture of three distinct world faith systems with a common and storied origin—is incalculable.

—*Rediscovering the Sacred*, 128 and 130

* * *

God of the snake, God of the cross,
how shall
we sing
your song
in a strange
land?

—*The Shaping of a Life*, 259 (prose in the original)

MODERN SPIRITUAL MASTERS
Robert Ellsberg, Series Editor

This series introduces the essential writing and vision of some of the great spiritual teachers of our time. While many of these figures are rooted in long-established traditions of spirituality, others have charted new, untested paths. In each case, however, they have engaged in a spiritual journey shaped by the challenges and concerns of our age. Together with the saints and witnesses of previous centuries, these modern spiritual masters may serve as guides and companions to a new generation of seekers.

Already published:

Modern Spiritual Masters (edited by Robert Ellsberg)
Swami Abhishiktananda (edited by Shirley du Boulay)
Metropolitan Anthony of Sourozh (edited by Gillian Crow)
Eberhard Arnold (edited by Johann Christoph Arnold)
Pedro Arrupe (edited by Kevin F. Burke, S.J.)
Daniel Berrigan (edited by John Dear)
Thomas Berry (edited by Mary EvelynTucker and John Grim)
Dietrich Bonhoeffer (edited by Robert Coles)
Robert McAfee Brown (edited by Paul Crowley)
Dom Helder Camara (edited by Francis McDonagh)
Carlo Carretto (edited by Robert Ellsberg)
G. K. Chesterton (edited by William Griffin)
Joan Chittister (edited by Mary Lou Kownacki
and Mary Hembrow Snyder)
Yves Congar (edited by Paul Lakeland)
The Dalai Lama (edited by Thomas A. Forsthoefel)
Alfred Delp, S.J. (introduction by Thomas Merton)
Catherine de Hueck Dogerty (edited by David Meconi, S.J.)
Virgilio Elizondo (edited by Timothy Matovina)
Charles de Foucauld (edited by Robert Ellsberg)
Mohandas Gandhi (edited by John Dear)
Bede Griffiths (edited by Thomas Matus)
Romano Guardini (edited by Robert A. Krieg)
Gustavo Gutiérrez (edited by Daniel G. Groody)

Thich Nhat Hanh (edited by Robert Ellsberg)
Abraham Joshua Heschel (edited by Susannah Heschel)
Etty Hillesum (edited by Annemarie S. Kidder)
Caryll Houselander (edited by Wendy M. Wright)
Pope John XXIII (edited by Jean Maalouf)
Rufus Jones (edited by Kerry Walters)
Clarence Jordan (edited by Joyce Hollyday)
John Main (edited by Laurence Freeman)
Anthony de Mello (edited by William Dych, S.J.)
Thomas Merton (edited by Christine M. Bochen)
John Muir (edited by Tim Flinders)
John Henry Newman (edited by John T. Ford, C.S.C.)
Henri Nouwen (edited by Robert A. Jonas)
Flannery O'Connor (edited by Robert Ellsberg)
Karl Rahner (edited by Philip Endean)
Brother Roger of Taizé (edited by Marcello Fidanzio)
Oscar Romero (by Marie Dennis, Rennie Golden, and Scott Wright)
Albert Schweitzer (edited by James Brabazon)
Frank Sheed and Maisie Ward (edited by David Meconi)
Sadhu Sundar Singh (edited by Charles E. Moore)
Mother Maria Skobtsova (introduction by Jim Forest)
Dorothee Soelle (edited by Dianne L. Oliver)
Edith Stein (edited by John Sullivan, O.C.D.)
David Steindl-Rast (edited by Clare Hallward)
William Stringfellow (edited by Bill Wylie-Kellerman)
Pierre Teilhard de Chardin (edited by Ursula King)
Mother Teresa (edited by Jean Maalouf)
St. Thérèse of Lisieux (edited by Mary Frohlich)
Henry David Thoreau (edited by Tim Flinders)
Howard Thurman (edited by Mary Krohlich)
Leo Tolstoy (edited by Charles E. Moore)
Evelyn Underhill (edited by Emilie Griffin)
Jean Vanier (edited by Carolyn Whitney-Brown)
Swami Vivekananda (edited by Victor M. Parachin)
Simone Weil (edited by Eric O. Springsted)
John Howard Yoder (edited by Paul Martens and Jenny Howells)